HONG KONG

by Ruth Lor M
with photograph
Magnus Bartlett, Jacky Yip
& Airphoto International Ltd.

With an Introduction by
Richard Hughes

A South China **SCMP** Morning Post Publication

Published by South China Morning Post Ltd.
Publications Division.
Morning Post Building,
Tong Chong Street,
Quarry Bay,
Hong Kong.

Printed by Yee Tin Tong Printing Press Ltd.
Tong Chong Street,
Quarry Bay,
Hong Kong.

Produced by Odyssey Productions Ltd.

Acknowledgements
    The experience of many Hong Kong residents has made this book
possible. I am especially indebted to: Joan Ahrens, Jim Browning, Bud
Carroll, May Chan, Rose Chan (of the Macau Tourist Information Bureau),
Enid Harper, Rosalind Henwood, Monique Hochstrasser, Robert and Cathy
Keatley, Linda, Martin and Terry Malloy, Matt Miller, Vyvyan Tenorio, David
Napoleon, Stephen and Evelyn Peplow, Jane Ram, Cam Sharrill, Pat
Sephton, Ritsu Spaeth, The Up Club, Ellen Van Dusen, Frances Yuen and
Lucy Zavelle.
    I am also grateful for the generous assistance of International Tourism,
Watertours, Hong Kong's many top hotels, Hong Kong Government
information offices, the Tung Wah Group of Hospitals, Citibank, the Royal
Hong Kong Jockey Club, and especially the Hong Kong Tourist Association.

ISBN 962-10-0014-9
                                                    Printed in Hong Kong

4

Contents

Introduction 8
    Geography 13
    History 13
    Government 16
    People 17
    Religion 17
    Language 18
General Information 19
    Climate 19
    When to Go 19
    What to Pack 20
    Immigration 20
    Customs 21
    Arriving By Sea, By Air 21
    Leaving Hong Kong 22
    Health 22
    Money 23
    Tipping 23
    Communications 24
    Media 25
    Transport 25
    Shopping 32
    Tourist Services 41
    Hotels 41
    Children 45
Sports and Recreation 47
    Horse Racing 49
    Keeping Fit 51
Arts and Entertainment 52
    Movies 53
    Television 53
    Museums 53
    Chinese Opera 55
    Nightlife 56
    Festivals 60
Food and Drink 64
    Dim Sum 66
    Regional Cuisines 68
    Desserts and Drinks 69
    Adventurous Eating 72

Things to See and Do 73
  Hong Kong Island 73
  Hong Kong Harbour 81
  Stanley Market 89
  Sung Dynasty Village 95
  Macau 96
  China 104
  Other Excursions 109
  Lantau 111
  Tram Ride 112
  A Bus Tour Around the Island 116
  Tiger Balm Gardens 116
  Yau Ma Tei Walking Tour 116
  Bird Market 120
  Chinese Gods, Chinese Temples 121
  Man Mo Temple 124
Recommended Reading 128
Appendix 129
Index 139

Prices throughout are quoted in Hong Kong dollars.

Introduction

Hong Kong is the last important colonial remnant of the once-mighty British Empire. Its population (around 5.5 million) comprises nearly ninety per cent of the thirteen colonies still bowing to London.

And now the future — as all visitors will discover — is the question dominating all local discussions.

The so-called 'lease' expires in 1997 when China, in the opinion of all those whose judgement I value, will of course take over.

Why should there be any surprise? Hong Kong is China. It is a borrowed place living on borrowed time and has survived as an impudent capitalist colony on China's communist derriere because it suits China.

Instead of pursuing Comrade Karl Marx's socialist ideals of 'life, liberty and the pursuit of happiness,' it has insisted on '*hard* life, *trade* liberty and the pursuit of *capital*.'

But the Chinese — being Chinese first and communists a poor second — will not change the basic structure, free trade operations and social life of the Hong Kong settlement, which has been hailed by so many economists as their favourite example of the advantage of private industry unfettered by government.

Every official statement by Beijing, gloating over the end of the lease, asserts that Hong Kong's 'continuing stability and prosperity will be preserved.' China has tolerated British sovereignty over Hong Kong since the lease was signed, although there have been some clashes. In 1956, when I arrived to make it my base as a barefoot reporter in the Far East, there were communal street riots — not because of my arrival, but in protest against bus and ferry fare increases.

And in 1967 there was the only real upheaval, which was provoked by the 'Red Guards' (revolutionary Chinese youth groups), who stormed through Hong Kong.

Signs appeared in the streets: 'Slaughter white-skin pigs!' Communist-owned department stores selling Chinese-made products became clandestine bomb-assembly centres. Bomb threats were directed against the Western tourist trade, repeatedly against the downtown Hilton Hotel, and two powerful bombs exploded inside the building.

On the roof of Beijing's Bank of China building, opposite the hotel, communist bankers, understandably anxious to display their comradely ultra-leftism (while secretly groaning over loss of capitalist profits), hoisted a huge neon sign: 'Chairman Mao — Live 10,000 Years!'

The Bank of China staff, on the building's top verandah, next door to the capitalist Hongkong and Shanghai Bank, used to fling stones and bottles at passersby in the streets below.

But eventually the turmoil ended. It had gained nothing for China. On the contrary, it had lost China valuable trade.

Beijing — significantly — was angered by the rioting, and privately apologised to the British Embassy.

Speculation about the future of Hong Kong should be governed by recollections that in those old days Beijing realised that a stable and prosperous Hong Kong was essential for Hong Kong's welfare and people, and for China's advantage.

Today, the 17-mile border between Hong Kong and China is already vanishing both politically and financially.

Chinese army units and Hong Kong's army garrison and police security forces cooperate in preventing illegal immigrants from sneaking into Hong Kong.

The so-called 'Special Economic Zone' of Shenzhen, up against the border, has been granted virtually autonomous rule and trade by Beijing, and is already attracting heavy foreign investment from Hong Kong. China's first golf course — to help attract foreign-devil tourists — will be built, under Hong Kong advice, in Shenzhen.

Foreign investments are spreading throughout Guangdong province. By early 1983, the province had received more than one billion US dollars in foreign investment.

Astonishingly, in an under-reported deal, China has 'purchased' some of its own sacred soil inside Hong Kong's leased New Territories for capitalist-style construction and development. Shenzhen authorities are now persuading a Hong Kong land investment company to sell burial plots to overseas Chinese who wish to return to eternity in their homeland.

One Hong Kong China-watcher has pointed out: 'The province's motto can be summed up simply: Investors wanted — dead or alive!'

In Hong Kong itself, the most visible signs of China's new accord with capitalism are the numerous communist department stores, banks and restaurants. Hong Kong is now the source, or 'entry-point', of about one-third of China's total foreign earnings — and accordingly indispensable in a continuing decadent-capitalist shape, say most economists, if China is to meet its own modernisation and turn-of-the-century targets.

Perhaps an ancient sign, written in English and standing above the front window of a Chinese emporium in Hong Kong from 1945 until the end of last year, best summarised relations between China and Hong Kong: 'MUTUAL PROFIT'.

Maybe it will now be re-exhibited in Chinese, or (better still) in both Chinese and English.

It is amusing to recall that those involved in the British sovereignty seizure of Hong Kong island in the 1841 'opium war' were denounced and punished by the British government.

The new development at Tsim Sha Tsui East

On the British side (the winners), the honest man responsible, Trade Superintendent Captain Charles Elliot, RN, was sacked for bad judgement with good intentions, and ended up in exile, first as Consul-General to Texas and then as Governor of St. Helena.

On the Chinese side (the losers), the honest man personally responsible, Commissioner Lin Tse-hsu, and the dishonest man personally responsible, High Commissioner Kishen, were sacked for bad judgement with bad intentions, and banished respectively to Siberia and Tibet.

Kishen and Elliot, in later years, remembered each other with compassion and respect.

'Poor devil,' said Elliot of Kishen on St. Helena. 'I suppose the Emperor beheaded him.'

'Elliot was an honest man,' said Kishen in Tibet. 'I hear that Queen Victoria beheaded him.'

Young Queen Victoria wrote: 'All we wanted we might have got if it had not been for the unacceptably strange conduct of Chas. Elliot. He tried to obtain the lowest terms from the Chinese.'

Viscount Palmerston, then Foreign Secretary, wrote to Elliot: 'You have disobeyed and neglected your instructions; you have deliberately abstained from first employing the armed forces placed at your disposal; and you have accepted terms which fall far short of those you were instructed to obtain.

'You have obtained the cession of Hong Kong, a bare island with hardly a house on it. Now it seems obvious that Hong Kong will not be a mart for trade.'

In Beijing, the Imperial Dragon — the Emperor — appropriated Kishen's personal property, worth ten million pounds sterling, and wrote with his vermilion brush:

'After Kishen arrived in Canton, he willingly succumbed to the wiles of the rebel barbarian ... Hong Kong is an important place. Kishen has allowed the rebels to occupy it officially. A misdemeanour so high shows indeed that he has no conscience.

'Let him be deprived of his post and imprisoned.'

I suppose Queen Victoria and Lord Palmerston would concede today that they were wrong and the Imperial Dragon was right.

Hong Kong's success story, by general agreement, was best summed up by Attorney-General John Griffiths, Q.C., who retired in 1983 after five year's service.

He listed the title tributes of recent authors:

'An Economic Nature Reserve', 'Borrowed Place Living On Borrowed Time', 'A Shop Window of the Free Way of Life in Asia', 'Capitalist Paradise', 'A Living Fossil of Early Imperial Government', 'A Rumbling Volcano', 'A Shopper's Paradise', 'A Commercial Miracle', 'Emporium of the East', 'The Home of *Laissez-Faire*'.

Then he quoted 'the figures which speak for themselves': Hong Kong is now the third largest container port, not just in Asia, but in the world; its gold and silver exchange has become the world's third largest gold-dealing centre; the presence of 128 licensed banks, including the giants from every leading and indeed secondary financial nation, has made it the financial capital of Asia, exceeded only by New York and London as a banking and financial centre.

'What was the secret behind the success?' Mr Griffiths asked.

'There is no doubt that the accident of geography had something to do with it, allowing that "barren rock" to become not merely the entrepôt of the China trade, but at the same time one of the most active trading cities in the world, and indeed the financial capital of Asia.'

Extraordinary things can happen to you when you visit the Far East. They tend to make you feel that you are becoming susceptible to Chinese superstition — which persists in China even after communist 'liberation'.

I first visited Shanghai in 1940. On my second visit in 1956 — when I was labouring as a barefoot reporter in China until 1957 — I naturally had a sad look at the changed landmarks and ancient monuments which I had first sighted in 1940: The Shanghai Club, the Bund, the Cathay and Park hotels, Broadway Mansions, etcetera, etcetera.

Escorted of course by my alleged Chinese party guide (but really guard) I strolled across the zig-zag bridge near Shanghai's old 'Secret Garden' and encountered one of the Chinese fortune-tellers who were still allowed to operate. My guide-guard condescendingly agreed to interpret his evaluation of my hand.

He astounded me by pointing out that I had first visited Shanghai sixteen years before — not known even to my guide-guard — and then said that I would be leaving China in early 1957 (which didn't surprise me), but assured me that I would be returning after another sixteen years. He repeated sixteen years.

Believe it or not, so I did in 1973, quite unexpectedly, to attend a first British trade fair in Beijing, to which foreign correspondents, including *The Times*, had of course to be admitted.

An improbable coincidence over those 'sixteens', I still think. When I went back to Shanghai on that third visit on 1973, there were no fortune-tellers on the bridge. Visitors to Hong Kong can still find them. But I am too frightened now to seek their forecasts.

My 1956 fortune-teller had given me another tip, which I used in the 1975 re-visit to enliven a fleeting interview with then Prime Minister Chou En-lai.

The fortune-teller had pointed out that the tip of each of my little fingers rose above the top joint of the third finger.

'This means,' he said, 'that you can rely upon your friends,' adding that he had once read Chairman Mao's hands and discovered that he was blessed with especially long fingers.

On my 1975 visit, our gang of invited correspondents was led in procession past Chou En-lai for a brief exchange of good wishes, but with instructions not to ask any newspaper questions. As we shook hands, I said: 'Mr Premier, may I see your little fingers?'

The startled interpreter, quite unnecessary for interpretation, was shaken, but the Premier immediately extended his palms, which showed very long little fingers.

'I see you believe in our Chinese superstition, Mr Hughes,' Chou En-lai remarked in perfect English, with a chuckle.

'I have learned a lot in my years in China, Mr Premier,' I said, bowing and moving on.

'Remember, Mr Hughes,' he called to me, 'we politicians need long little fingers much more than you journalists do.'

I reckon that China in 1997 will be studying its own long little fingers hopefully, because their length would mean that it could 'rely upon its friends' — one of which would have to be Hong Kong.

Geography

Hong Kong consists of 236 islands and a peninsula attached to the China mainland, making a total land area of 1,061.7 sq.km. It is divided up administratively into Hong Kong Island, Kowloon, and the New Territories.

In spite of the popular image of tall buildings and sailing junks, 70 per cent of the land is woodland, grass and scrub. Only 9 per cent is intensely developed, with some buildings reaching a height of 66 storeys. Some of the islands are not even inhabited. The population is concentrated around the rim of Hong Kong Island, in Kowloon and, increasingly, in the new towns of the New Territories.

Most of the rest is mountainous, with 20 peaks reaching more than 344 metres and two more than 900 metres. Next year the number may be fewer: mountains here have a tendency to disappear. Since the earliest British beginnings mountains have been used as 'infill' for land reclamation schemes. The original shoreline on Hong Kong Island, for example, was along Queen's Road Central, three blocks from where it is now.

Hong Kong Island itself is dominated by the Peak, which rises sharply over the forest of towering buildings above the harbour. Kowloon, across the water, is lined with the airport, ocean ship passenger terminals, luxury apartments and hotels, shopping centres and industrial buildings. Beyond it, in the haze, rise the 'Eight Dragons', the eight hills after which Kowloon, the Nine Dragons, is named. The Ninth Dragon, so the story goes, was the young Sung emperor.

History

The oldest archaeological finds indicate that there was some human activity here around 4000 B.C. The earliest people were probably of Malay-Oceanic origin and boat-dwellers. The earliest known structure is the impressive **Han Dynasty Tomb** in Lei Chung Uk in Kowloon, built around 100-150 A.D. The earliest records of land tenure are from the Sung dynasty (960-1279 A.D.). At the end of that dynasty the youthful emperor, fleeing from the Mongols, took temporary refuge in the Kowloon area, near to the present-day site of Kai Tak airport.

The first Europeans in the area were the Portuguese who settled in Macau, 64 km. away, in 1557. The Spanish, Dutch, English and French followed, mainly traders, sailors and missionaries. In 1757 foreign men were allowed to reside in Whampoa, just outside Canton, during the October-May trading season. It was here that most of the tea and silk trade with China was negotiated. For the remainder of the year, the foreigners were confined to Macau.

These restrictions and the refusal of China to behave in the manner of a western trading nation frustrated the British traders in particular. They consequently came to see the acquisition of a British-controlled island off the China coast as essential for the growth of trade. By then, opium was openly traded.

Opium was first smoked in China in the 17th century and rapidly caught on as a recreational drug. In the 18th century the Chinese government, concerned about the effects of drug addiction, started to restrict the supply. For the British who brought it from India, opium was solving balance-of-payment problems, and traders refused to heed Chinese appeals to stop.

In 1839 Lin Zixu, a forthright imperial commissioner, seized all the opium in the hands of foreign traders in Whampoa and laid siege to foreign 'factories' there. His men burned more than 20,000 chests of the narcotic, almost a year's trade. The British withdrew, first to Macau, and then to Hong Kong harbour. Tension mounted. The British fleet with its superior fire-power was called in, and the **First Opium War** scored a direct entry into the pages of the history books.

With China's defeat Hong Kong was ceded to Britain, and the Union Jack was raised on January 26, 1841 on Possession Point. The British Government, however, did not recognise its new colony until June 1843. It was, complained Lord Palmerston, the British Foreign Secretary, just a 'barren island with hardly a house on it'.

Contrary to Lord Palmerston's complaint, Hong Kong Island was host to more than a few houses. Its population was about 4,000 in 1841, quickly growing to 23,872 in 1847. Ambitious immigrants from both China and beyond were attracted by the fortunes to be made, and the new colony became a haven for refugees fleeing revolutions and uprisings in their own lands. In 1941 the government counted 1.6 million mouths.

The Japanese attacked Hong Kong at about the same time as Pearl Harbour, overcoming the resisting British, Canadian and Chinese forces on Christmas Day, 1941. The British regained control in August 1945. During the Japanese occupation the population dwindled to about 600,000 as many residents fled to the relative safety of the Chinese interior. They returned after the war and by 1947 the population stood at 1.8 million.

The civil war between the communists and the nationalists, culminating in the 1949 takeover by the communists, led to an enormous influx of refugees. Some years later half a million people arrived from China, fleeing the excesses of the Cultural Revolution. Like earlier migrants many swam, hired boats or crept in on foot.

In 1966 the Cultural Revolution erupted in China and reached Hong Kong a year later in the form of anti-British riots and bombings. Some violent demonstrations took place, several at the foot of Garden Road near the Hilton Hotel. Loudspeakers on the Bank of China building blared out communist slogans. Property values sank. Order, however, was restored by the end of the year.

Until October 1980 the Hong Kong government allowed any Chinese to stay if he or she could manage to 'touch base'; that is, reach the urban areas undetected. Those caught were fed and repatriated the next morning. However, because of the tremendous increase in people, services like housing and health care deteriorated. Laws were passed requiring everyone aged 15 and over to carry identification at all times. The regulations are quite fierce: it is an offence to employ an illegal immigrant ('II'). Anyone who aids and abets an illegal immigrant, even a close relative, is prosecuted. Despite all this the numbers are still growing. The 1981 census counted 5.1 million people including 34,506 Vietnamese refugees.

Links with China are necessarily close. Hong Kong is the source of 40 per cent of China's foreign exchange, and a major market for Chinese produce of all types. In addition, many residents lived in China either under its feudalist or, later, under its communist systems.

In spite of limited arable land and ceaseless waves of immigrants, Hong Kong has more than just survived. In the early eighties when a recession hit the world, it was still one of the liveliest cities imaginable. Old buildings continued to be replaced with new skyscrapers built at a pace unequalled anywhere else in the world. In 1981 (one of Hong Kong's headiest years) 603 new buildings with a total usable floor area of 3,186,514 square metres were completed.

The formula for success? Luck, adaptability, hard work and entrepreneurial skills and capital, especially from Shanghai refugees. British order and the existence of China next door is all that need be added.

Government

Hong Kong has a governor (currently Sir Edward Youde) who lives in a loosely guarded white mansion in the Mid-Levels, with a vast garden, opened once a year so the people can enjoy the azaleas in bloom. The governor represents the British crown and approves all bills passed by the Legislative Council whose members are appointed by London.

In 1952 popular elections were first held for seats on the Urban Council, a relatively low-level body which administers such services as markets, playgrounds and liquor licences. Since 1982 Hong Kong has also elected members to its district boards. In these, elected representatives join with government officials and appointed citizens to consider issues and propose policy changes on a fairly wide level.

Although many of its critics may not agree, the government is reasonably sensitive to the demands of its people and in this part of the world is one of the greatest exponents of personal liberty. As a result, the Chinese majority, many of whom risked their lives to leave the stifling economic atmosphere of China, are not clamouring for independence or a return to Chinese rule.

The government is a paternalistic facilitator, the provider of a stable environment in which industry and commerce can flourish. There are no minimum wage laws, no foreign exchange controls and few import duties. Personal income tax is 15 per cent, business taxes only slightly more.

The People

Hong Kong's population is 98.1 per cent Chinese, mainly Cantonese. Most of the 'other nationals' are British, Indians, Americans, Japanese and Filipinos.

Forty-two per cent of the population live in government-subsidised housing. Free schooling is provided for nine years and subsidised schooling thereafter. It costs HK$3 to consult a doctor, take an X-ray, have a laboratory test or settle a prescription charge.

The Chinese, with their demanding family obligations, Confucian formality and busy lives, tend to socialise among themselves. Western foreigners (known collectively or singly and sometimes even affectionately as *gwailo* — 'foreign devils') also tend to stick to themselves. Relations between races, though far from intimate (except in cross-cultural marriages), have been good, although at Christmas, 1981 several *gwailos* were attacked on the street by a gang of undisciplined youths. But one outburst is not a trend.

Local residents are subject to many pressures: crowded flats, noisy neighbours and nearby construction and high rents. There is the daily competition for taxis, for space on buses, in stores and in restaurants. And behind all this lurks the worry of how 'the lease question' will be solved.

Because of tradition and because homes are usually very cramped, entertaining is often done in restaurants. While *gwailos* will split bills, Chinese hospitality will not allow such 'Dutchness', and meals may end with a fight over who pays. Chinese people live to eat, not eat to live, and any excuse for a good restaurant meal is grabbed. A gift is not expected but impressions of you improve if you don't arrive empty-handed. Most Chinese bring each other fruit (Sunkist oranges are a favourite because they look like big balls of gold) or imported Danish cookies. A foreigner might bring a souvenir from home.

Returning hospitality with hospitality is much appreciated. If you can afford it, invite your host to a restaurant in one of the top hotels.

Religion

Buddhism, Taoism, animism, Confucianism, ancestor worship and Christianity are among the religious beliefs followed in Hong Kong. Many boat people look to Tin Hau or Tam Kung for protection. Chinese people are pragmatists and want to be sure that all possible ways to success are covered.

Temple of 10,000 Buddhas at Shatin

Language

English and Cantonese are the official languages. Cantonese is tonal, like notes on a musical scale. Some say it has nine tones, some eleven. Whatever the case, it is not an easy language to learn. It is more difficult than Mandarin, the official language of mainland China. Tones are more important than consonants. The word *ma* said in one tone means something totally different in another, and you may be saying something insulting if you use the wrong tone. Words are of one syllable and sentences frequently get punctuated with a lot of elongated 'ah's. The written language is the same for all Chinese dialects so a Mandarin speaker is able to communicate with a Cantonese speaker in writing.

English is taught as a second language in most primary schools and is the language of instruction at Hong Kong University. Most stores in tourist shopping areas have at least one person who speaks English. But taxi and bus drivers can generally understand only the simplest of directions. Policemen who have passed an English-language proficiency test wear a red patch under the numbers on their epaulettes. Only the highly educated or post-1950 China-educated speak Mandarin.

General Information

Climate

The climate is most pleasant from September to early March. The rains have diminished, and the humidity is at its lowest. October through to February is sunny and pleasant, and good for hiking. Sweaters are needed on October evenings and in the daytime from November on. For cold spells in January and February top coats are essential, sometimes with linings, even during the day. Hong Kong matrons love this time, as it gives them an opportunity to show off their furs. Since homes are not usually centrally heated, warm indoor clothes are a necessity too.

March and April can be foggy at times, though high areas like the Peak may be foggy at any time of year. The rains start in earnest in March, with occasional days of sunshine interrupting weeks of intermittent rain and clouds. The mean annual rainfall is 2,225 mm., 80 per cent of this falling between May and September. June is the rainiest month, but it is not unpleasant, and the rains bring bold, dark clouds that turn the seascape into a beautiful black-and-white etching.

April through to September is typhoon and south-west monsoon season. 'Typhoon' is actually a Chinese word meaning 'great wind'. Typhoons blow up to 120 knots an hour, pouring water down like a bathroom shower for hours at a time. This is the time to stay indoors, as flowerpots, laundry poles and other dangerous missiles tend to fly off roofs and balconies. Almost everything stops for a storm signal No. 8, though the MTR runs on a limited schedule.

Not all typhoons are severe. An average of 13 'tropical cyclones' affect Hong Kong between July and October each year, and about two of these might have winds strong enough to make residents think about storm shutters, canned food and bottled water. Most typhoons and the monsoon just bring a lot of rain and inconvenience.

Hong Kong has a set of warning signals. Signal No. 3 gives 12 hours warning of strong winds. Signal No. 8 means winds with a speed of at least 34 knots within 12 hours, and a signal No.10 means a sustained wind speed of 64-120 knots. From 1971 to 1980 the signal No. 8 was hoisted 16 times, the dreaded No. 10 only three. A plotting map is provided in the local business telephone directory.

When to Go

Choice of season is very important — the summer months are so hot and humid that sightseeing is anything but pleasant. Apart from the weather, here are some other considerations:

The local schools are on holiday from mid-June to early September, so it's a time best avoided if you want a beach to yourself. Many expatriates go on home leave at this time, and local people like to travel during the summer. They also like to travel during the lunar New Year, Easter and Christmas vacations, thus jamming all means of transport in and out of the colony. Those who stay at home spend their weekends visiting many of the places you will wish to see. Be wary of far-flung or ambitious plans on Sundays all year round.

The general holidays (when offices, banks, schools and factories are closed) are: every Sunday; the first weekday in January; the first three days of the lunar New Year (end of January-early February); Easter (four days including Good Friday); Ching Ming (March-April); the Queen's Birthday (June 11); the Dragon Boat Festival (June); Liberation of Hong Kong Day (last Monday in August); Mid-Autumn Festival (September); Chung Yeung Festival (October); Christmas and the following two days.

Some festivals are based on the lunar calendar, and their dates fluctuate each year. Contact the Hong Kong Tourist Association for specific information.

What to Pack

During July and August light cottons are mandatory. Synthetics are too hot. The humidity can be oppressive, the temperature hovering around 33°C for days. The MTR (subway), most taxis, some of the ferries, and all important shops are air-conditioned. Restaurants can be so cold that wraps are recommended for bare female shoulders.

Visitors can dress casually most of the time, but should dress up for high class bars and restaurants. Businessmen wear suits and ties for most business appointments.

Immigration

Tourist visas are not necessary for most nationalities carrying valid travel documents, but you may be asked to show some means of support for your stay and/or travel tickets out of the colony. An immigration officer will stamp the length of stay permitted onto your passport: six months for most UK passport holders, three months for Commonwealth and some Western European and South American countries, and one month for other Western European, some South American and Asian countries and the U.S. A trip to Macau does not merit an additional period of stay in Hong Kong.

Further information and visas can be obtained from British consulates or high commissions abroad, or from the Information Office, Dept. of Immigration, 61 Mody Road, Tsim Sha Tsui East, Kowloon, telephone 3-7333111.

Customs

Taxes have to be paid if you import more than 200 cigarettes, 50 cigars or 250 gm. of tobacco, and 6 ml. of perfume or 250 ml. of toilet water. Tax will also have to be paid on more than one litre of alcohol. Passengers aged under 18 are not qualified for liquor and tobacco exemptions. Virtually everything else is tax-free.

Customs officers are also eagle-eyed for illegal drugs and endangered animal species, living or dead, in parts or whole.

Dogs and cats will also be seized unless they have just come from at least six month's residence in the United Kingdom, Ireland, New Zealand or Australia, and they have veterinarian health certificates dated within 14 days prior to arrival. Plants, dogs and cats can be kept in quarantine for a few days until the owners' departure. Contact the Agriculture and Fisheries Department, 393 Canton Road, 14th Floor, Kowloon, telephone 3-688111.

Arriving by Sea

Most cruise ships dock at the Ocean Terminal in Tsim Sha Tsui. Passengers on ferries to and from China usually go through Tai Kok Tsui near the Yau Ma Tei typhoon shelter in Kowloon, an easy ferry ride from Blake Pier in Central if necessary. The railway station is in Kowloon.

Arriving by Air

Kai Tak is one of the most thrilling airports in the world. Aircraft frequently make their final approaches on a route which takes them between buildings and almost between cars on the road. The runway is built on reclaimed land which juts out into the harbour. Be ready for the unpleasant smell which may hit you when you disembark.

There are free telephones in the arrival hall. Baggage carts can be taken outside to transportation. Peak periods are 2pm to 4pm, and 9pm to 11pm.

In the buffer hall, past customs, there is an area for reserving hotel rooms, changing money and booking transport without going through the crowded greeting area. Hotel transportation, hire-cars and taxis are available.

Public coaches leave from a small terminus near the exit to the rear of the greeting area. The 200 plies between Central (the Mandarin Hotel) and the airport, with stops at the Plaza and Excelsior hotels in Causeway Bay. The 201 runs between the airport and the Peking Road Terminal (near the Hong Kong and Marco Polo hotels) in Tsim Sha Tsui, stopping by several of the other hotels in the area. They leave every 15 to 20 minutes from 7.25am to 10.30pm and cost a maximum of HK$4.

Cruise ships berthed at the Ocean Terminal

Leaving Hong Kong

On the way out of Hong Kong, there is a HK$100 airport tax, payable only in Hong Kong dollars at the check-in counter. Peak departure hours are 11am to 6pm. Within the airport you can leave luggage, buy postage stamps, change money and do last-minute shopping, but prices of course are better in town. The airport has a strict security search, and carry-on luggage is checked for size. Check with your airline if you want to take anything larger than 9"x14"x22" into the cabin of the plane. As an anti-noise measure, Kai Tak permits few loudspeaker announcements. Consult the bulletin boards for boardings and departures. If you have a long wait, it is more comfortable to spend the time in the Hotel Regal Meridien, accessible by elevated walkway from the airport.

Health

There is little to worry about, but avoid foods that haven't been cooked, peeled, or carefully washed. Tap water is potable unless rationing is in force. Hygiene standards in the restaurants listed here are good. We have mentioned places where you should take precautions.

No precautions are necessary for such diseases as cholera or typhoid unless Hong Kong is declared a cholera or typhoid area. No health certificates are necessary.

Money

The Hong Kong dollar is legal tender here but many merchants will accept any hard currency in either cash or traveller's cheques. Hong Kong currency notes are printed either by the Hongkong and Shanghai Banking Corporation or the Chartered Bank in denominations of $10 (green), $50 (blue), $100 (pink), $500 and $1,000. The last two notes are especially large. Coins are in denominations of $1, $2 (scalloped edge) and $5 (like two coins welded together) — all silver coloured. 10¢, 20¢ (scalloped edge) and 50¢ coins are bronze, and some people may need a magnifying glass to read the numbers.

Banks open at 9.30 or 10am, Mondays to Fridays, with some banks closing at 3pm, and others as late as 6pm. Most are open on Saturday mornings.

Hong Kong currency can be freely imported or exported. Exchange rates fluctuate daily. As a rough guide, exchange rates for some major currencies in mid-1983 were:

	HK$		HK$
US$1	7.25	D. Mark 1	2.83
Can$1	5.88	F. Franc 1	.94
Aust$1	6.34	Swedish Krona 1	.92
Sterling	11.00	Dutch Guilder 1	2.52
Japanese yen	.03	Italian Lira 1	.0049
Malaysia $1	3.09	Singapore $1	3.40

Credit cards are widely but not always accepted. Some shops will offer a discount for cash payment, but no surcharge is added for the cards. Personal cheques drawn on Hong Kong banks are usually accepted by stores. Please note that tours and aeroplane tickets bought from China International Travel Service and CAAC here are usually paid for in Hong Kong cash. Traveller's cheques and credit cards are not accepted.

Tipping

Restaurants, bars and hotels generally add a 10 per cent service charge but it is customary to leave small change. Check your bill to see if the 10 per cent has been added. If not and you want to tip, give about 10-15 per cent. Hotel bellboys and porters expect HK$2 a bag. Special help from a hotel concierge is usually rewarded with a tip of paper money, HK$10 or more. Taxi drivers do not expect tips for short trips but five to 10 per cent is appropriate for long trips.

Communications

Telephone: Local telephones are numerous and efficient. Whether you get someone speaking English at the other end is something else. Most stores will allow you free local calls. Just ask, 'Deen hwa?' for 'telephone?'. Some public telephones requiring HK$1 coins are also available.

Telephone numbers are prefaced with area codes — '5' for Hong Kong Island and outlying islands, '3' for Kowloon, and '0' for New Territories.

For example, if you are calling 5-244106 from the airport you have to dial the '5' at the beginning. If you are calling 3-671111, a number that begins with the same area code as the telephone you are using, dial only the 671111.

Important Telephone Numbers

Police, Ambulance, Fire	999
Directory Enquiries	108
International Operator	100 or 101
Special Police Tourist Hotline — English, Chinese and Japanese-speaking	5-277177
Airport Information	3-829359
Community Advice Bureau — all kinds of help from baby-sitters to Hash House Harriers	5-245444
Consumer Council — information on authorised dealers and registration of complaints	5-748297
Cable and Wireless	5-2831233
Hong Kong Tourist Association Tourist Information	3-671111
Hong Kong Tourist Association — to check on memberships and register complaints	5-244106
Ocean Terminal	3-667721
Postal Enquiries	5-2671222
Weather Information	5-456381

Medical emergencies — contact the doctor in your hotel or go to the Emergency Service, Hong Kong Adventist Hospital. 40 Stubbs Road, tel. 5-746211.

Mail: Locally the Post Office aims at a 24-hour delivery service, usually with two deliveries a day.

A first class airmail letter reaches Britain in five days and the U.S. in seven. The faster but more expensive 'Express' and 'Speedpost' services are also available.

Cable and Wireless handles electronic international communications. Some homes, offices and hotels are registered for International Direct Dialling and other international telephoning services. You can usually send a cable from a subscriber telephone but not a pay telephone. Ask your hotel for help.

Cable and Wireless also handles Phototelegrams, Bureaufax, Ship-to-Shore and Air-Ground Communications. Its offices are next to the Furama Hotel, in the Lee Gardens Hotel, and in the Ocean Terminal in Tsim Sha Tsui.

Media

Hong Kong has six English-language daily newspapers. The most popular is the *South China Morning Post*. Others include the *Asian Wall Street Journal* and the Asian edition of the *International Herald Tribune;* the first is a business journal, the second of more general interest, particularly to Americans. Also printed locally is the *China Daily*, an English-language newspaper out of Beijing.

Several English-language radio stations give news headlines frequently, reporting the progress of typhoons very closely. **Commercial Radio** at 1044kHz gives news and weather bulletins every half hour with major bulletins at 8am, 12.30pm and 6.30pm. You can find the **BBC World News** at 7am or 7pm on **Radio 3** at 567kHz or **Radio 4** at 91mHz, 100.5mHz and 100.9mHz.

The main television news is on both English-language channels at 7pm with brief bulletins at 9.30pm and 11.10 or 11.15pm.

Transport

Note: Only a few taxi and bus drivers speak English. When travelling around on your own, be sure to have the name of your residence and destination in Chinese characters. The simplest way to stop a driver is to say *'nee doh'* meaning 'here', and *'lok cheh'* meaning 'get off the vehicle'.

Hong Kong has 330,309 registered vehicles for 1182 km. of roads, one of the highest traffic densities in the world. During rush hours, 7.30-9.30am and 5.30-7.30pm, count on a lot of extra time when travelling. Give yourself an extra hour to get through the Cross-Harbour Tunnel, just to be on the safe side.

For ferry and bus schedules, phone the HKTA, 3-671111.

Buses

Most are double-decked, and the upper storey is ideal for sightseeing. During peak hours, try to board at the bus terminus rather than a bus stop, particularly if you don't want to stand. The main terminals are close to the Star Ferries. The bus system covers most of the colony, with some routes serviced every three minutes, others once an hour, depending on demand. The fare is shown on the coin box near the driver. No change is given. To stop the bus, press the button or black rubber strip once. Testy drivers, annoyed by constantly ringing bells, will sometimes stop their buses and scold passengers. This apart, they will not usually speak, not even to announce a stop.

Bus riding is not too difficult. Destinations are posted on the front of the bus. Express coaches, identified by yellow labels with red letters, are more comfortable, cost more and take no standees. Buses with white lettering on red and numbered in the one hundreds go through the harbour tunnel. Most tunnel buses stop at the Hung Hom railway station.

Public Light Buses

Public light buses (PLBs) have the advantage of being able to stop almost anywhere except beside a yellow line on the road or sidewalk. No standing is allowed. The yellow ones with the green stripes have fixed routes, schedules and fares. Fares for the red ones are not fixed and they will not usually move from a terminal until full. Both types of buses have their destinations and prices listed at the front. Pay as you are getting on (green) or getting off (red).

Ferries

Ferries are not just a romantic way to see Hong Kong, they are sometimes the fastest. For example, to go from Shaukeiwan to Kwun Tong takes only 10 minutes by ferry. By bus and MTR it might take over an hour and cost five times as much. There are about 16 cross-harbour ferry services, three of them carrying cars and trucks.

Fifteen additional services operate to the outlying islands. Some of these have a 'deluxe' class with air-conditioning, tables and a snack bar. The fare is no more than HK$8 one way, and is slightly cheaper on weekdays. The Outlying Islands ferry terminal is a five-minute walk to the right as you leave the Star Ferry on Hong Kong Island, just beyond the main bus terminal.

The Star Ferry

The famous Star Ferry was started in 1898. Before the MTR was built it was the fastest and most popular transport between Central and Tsim Sha Tsui, and usually played a part in every movie made in Hong Kong. It supplies the best view of Victoria Peak and shuttles between Edinburgh Place (near the Mandarin Hotel and City Hall) and Kowloon Point (Ocean Terminal and Star House) between 6.30am and 11.30pm and at intervals of between three and 20 minutes as demand requires. When the Star Ferry has stopped running, try the MTR, a bus or a walla-walla.

Motorised Boats

Walla-wallas are small covered motor boats that can be hired at Blake Pier or the Kowloon Public Pier, both next to the Star Ferry terminals. Other small boats can be hired at most harbours, and can be cheaper than hiring a junk for sightseeing, or for travelling between ship and shore. It pays to haggle before you board. Aberdeen is more expensive than other harbours because of the many tourists. See also 'Things to See and Do', page 73.

Mass Transit Railway

The Mass Transit Railway is not called the 'subway' or 'metro' or 'tube' here although that's what it is. Here it's the 'MTR' *('day ha tee')*. It is not only the fastest way to travel, it is also the most comfortable. Clean, bright and relatively crime free, its announcements are in both English and Cantonese. The system is currently shaped like a wildly dancing 'Y'. The main line goes from Central to Admiralty on Hong Kong Island, under the harbour to Tsim Sha Tsui, under Nathan Road, and then to Tsuen Wan in West Kowloon. This 16-station trip takes 28 minutes. The cross-harbour Admiralty to Tsim Sha Tsui segment takes about three minutes. Any other trip past Argyle or Prince Edward necessitates a change at one of these two stations.

The current system of 25 stations is 26.1 km. long. A guidebook and an MTR tourist brochure can be obtained free from the office in each station.

The price for each destination is prominently posted. Machines or staff dispense tickets and change. At the turnstiles, feed your plastic, credit-card-style ticket into the machine and then take back your ticket. Fight the impulse to snap the ticket. Its mutilation means a HK$1,000 fine. To get past the turnstiles after your train journey, feed the ticket into another machine.

Each station has a map and well-marked signs in English and Chinese to various exits. In some stations, you can walk for about a kilometre in air-conditioning, avoiding crowded, humid streets above. Trains currently run every two-and-a-half minutes during peak hours and three to five minutes otherwise. The system starts up at 6am and closes down at 1.15am. A discount-priced 'stored value' ticket, good for 90 days, will give you cheaper fares during off-peak hours. For more information, phone 3-7500170.

Trams

Trams operate only on Hong Kong Island from Kennedy Town, past Whitty Street and Western Market to Causeway Bay, North Point and Shaukeiwan. A branch line runs to Happy Valley. Central and Wanchai are between Western Market and Causeway Bay. If you avoid the Happy Valley tram, you can't get lost. All other trams run parallel to the harbour. Since they are cheap (50¢ flat fare), and are usually faster than walking, many people use them for short trips. They are, however, not meant for tall people.

The tram system was first built in 1904 and currently has 163 double-decker and 20 single-decker cars, some still with cool, wicker seats. Entrance is via the rear door and payment made as you exit in front. No change is given. Many trams are on the road from 6.30am to 11.45pm. Trams can be hired for parties and are fun for the sightseer. For more information, phone 5-8918765. See also 'Things to See and Do', page 73.

The Peak Tram

The Peak Tram runs from a terminus on Garden Road, just a short walk up from the Hilton Hotel. It is part of the public transport system and is surprisingly cheap for a major tourist attraction. It runs from 7am to midnight. For information phone 5-8918765 or 5-220922. See also 'Things to See and Do, Day One', page 73.

Taxis

Taxis are usually hailed on the streets, except in very congested areas. You can also queue up for them at big hotels, the Star Ferry terminals, Admiralty MTR station, the airport and train station. Urban taxis are red with grey roofs, while New Territories taxis are green. Most taxis have driver-controlled doors and air-conditioning. Some have two-way radios, helpful if the driver speaks no English. His dispatcher at the other end of the radio usually speaks English. All taxis have meters and lighted 'taxi' signs on top when available for hire. Drivers are breaking the law if they refuse customers while the sign is lit.

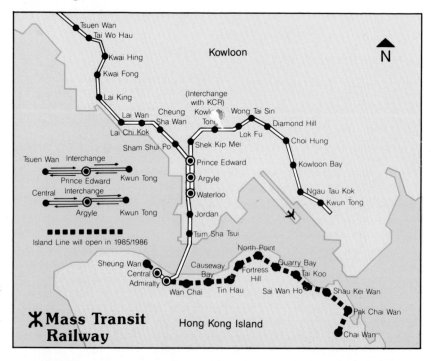

Taxi drivers at the airport are notorious for trying to get more than they deserve. They have been known to ignore the decimal point on their meters, asking HK$125 for a HK$12.50 ride for example. Some will argue for a surcharge on a post-midnight pick-up. Don't pay it. Get help from the staff of your hotel, take down their licence numbers, and call the police.

The fare is HK$4.50 for the first two kilometres and 90 cents for each subsequent .45 km. For the New Territories, the first two km. cost HK$3. HK$10 extra is added for going through the Cross-Harbour Tunnel, HK$2 for the Aberdeen Tunnel, and HK$2 for the Lion Rock Tunnel. A charge of 50¢ is made for each bag. If a fare increase materialises after the time of going to press, the new prices will be posted prominently in the taxi, or the driver will have a card converting the meter reading to the new fares.

Kowloon taxi drivers are often reluctant to go to Hong Kong and vice versa. Many don't know the other side of the harbour. They especially don't like going there, or anywhere out of the way, just before their 3.30-4.30pm driver changeover. Drivers will cover their meters to indicate that they are not available. Kowloon taxis that cruise around the Excelsior and Plaza hotels might charge only half the regular tunnel price to get back through the tunnel to Kowloon.

During off-peak hours, you have a fair chance of obtaining a taxi by telephone. Look in the Yellow Pages. It is sometimes possible to hire a taxi by the hour.

Train

The Kowloon-Canton Railway (KCR) operates from a railway station at Hung Hom, adjacent to Tsim Sha Tsui East. The line is currently being electrified to Lo Wu on the border. When the line is completed, the 34 km. trip to the border will take 40 minutes. Train stops are at Mongkok, Kowloon Tong (change to MTR if desired here), Shatin, Chinese University, Taipo Kau, Taipo Market, Fan Ling, Sheung Shui and Lo Wu — in that order. Lo Wu is normally only open to documented China-bound passengers.

Rickshaws

Rickshaws are an endangered species. About 30 of these man-drawn two-wheeled carts still exist and some can be hired at either Star Ferry terminal. Most of the pullers are elderly, and those who retire are not being replaced. Don't feel too sorry for them.

They charge HK$5 to HK$20 for a three-minute ride or picture-taking session depending on whim. Establish the price before you climb aboard.

Shopping

Shopping in Hong Kong is superlative for several reasons. All imports are duty-free except for tobacco, perfume, cosmetics, alcohol, most motor vehicles and some petroleum products. There is no added-on sales tax, and many merchants aim for only a 10 per cent mark-up. They rely on volume to cover expenses and produce a profit, and outlay little for inventory and storage space.

Hong Kong also has a very large and affluent local market, and competition between retailers is fierce. The Hong Kong Tourist Association lists 220 jewellery stores and 38 camera stores among its 1,300 retail members, who form only a fraction of the stores available. Some businesses provide name cards with a 'memo' space for noting prices. Comparison shopping is expected.

Australian opals are cheaper here than in Australia because of tax differences. Japanese tourists find their own cameras cheaper than at home for the same reason. Americans find U.S.-made products cost about the same or slightly more than they are used to because of freight costs but are pleased with the prices of European and Asian-made goods. The more labour-intensive the cheaper the product compared to Europe and America.

Another advantage of Hong Kong, particularly over its neighbours, is the consumer protection. The Hong Kong Tourist Association has strict membership requirements and continually monitors restaurants and stores for knowledgeable staff, reasonable prices and good business practices. All gold sold by members has to have company and gold content marks stamped on it. Member establishments display a red and black sailing junk decal in their windows.

Both the HKTA and the Diamond Importers Association (DIA) will mediate disagreements between members and the rare dissatisfied customer. The government-sponsored Consumer Council will do the same with stores which are not members of the HKTA. Membership in the HKTA and DIA is so valued that clerks in non-member stores will lie that they are members. When in doubt, telephone the HKTA at 5-244191 or the DIA at 5-235497.

The HKTA gives out a free copy of its *Hong Kong Official Guidebook*. It is worth referring to for phone numbers and addresses of its members.

Hong Kong also sells goods from mainland China at prices lower than those in China itself. Chinese goods are sold all over Hong Kong but prices are particularly good in China products specialty stores. Look first in the Chinese Arts and Crafts stores for the best in Chinese jewellery, embroidered silks, jade carvings, cloisonne, porcelain, paintings, flowers made of gems and other luxury items. These stores are at Wyndham Street and Queen's Road in Central, in the New World Centre, at the Jordan Road MTR stop (233 Nathan Road), and in Star House by the Kowloon Star Ferry.

China products stores are more proletarian but equally exciting. Go there first and jot down prices and quality before venturing elsewhere. Prices are especially good if you go to the Overseas Chinese Service Department with your passport to get a 10 per cent discount privilege card.

The best of these stores are **Yue Hwa** at 301 Nathan Road, Kowloon (Jordan Road MTR stop), **Chinese Products Company** at 488 Hennessy

Antique and curio shop in Hollywood Road

Road near the Plaza Hotel in Causeway Bay, the **Chinese Merchandise Emporium** at 92-94 Queen's Road Central, and the **Chinese Goods Centre** at 395 King's Road, North Point. (They have many of the items also available at the **Chinese Arts and Crafts** stores, and sometimes cheaper.) These sell almost everything: silk and cotton yard goods, silk brocade-covered photo albums, luggage, beaded or cashmere sweaters, padded jackets, down quilts and jackets, porcelain, sports equipment, cloisonne vases, herbal medicines, rather plain everyday clothing, and lots of cheap, exotic items that are good as souvenirs for friends at home. A stop in their supermarkets if only to sightsee can be fascinating. All kinds of dried fruit and vegetables, teas, frozen camel's hump, liquors and wines tempt the inquisitive.

In addition, Hong Kong produces goods of its own that are exported abroad: more watches than Switzerland, more toys than Japan, designer name brand clothes, textiles, radios, calculators, luggage, porcelain, carpets, brassware, handbags and jewellery. This means that you can buy factory over-runs, seconds, and even some top-quality wares at pre-export prices.

Luxury Shopping

If time is short, money no deterrent, and tastes very discriminating, then reliable quality, luxury-class goods from all over the world are available at any of the following:

The **Peninsula Hotel** shopping arcades and shops along lower Nathan Road in Tsim Sha Tsui (**Design Thai, Via Condotti, Cartier, Charles Jourdan,** etc.); **The Landmark** (shopping centre) in Central (**Joyce's Boutique, Van Laack, Mario Valentino,** etc.); **Lane Crawford,** the top department store, in Central, Causeway Bay and Tsim Sha Tsui.

For **antiques,** browse along Hollywood Road and Wyndham Street in Central district.

A less exclusive department store is **Sincere** in Central. Try also the Japanese department stores in Causeway Bay which have a wide range of goods from many countries: **Daimaru, Matsuzakaya** and **Mitsukoshi.** The **Ocean Centre/Ocean Terminal/Harbour City/Hong Kong Hotel** complex in Tsim Sha Tsui offers hundreds of stores from which to choose.

Bargain Hunting

For top bargains you need much more time, but some of these can be covered in three hours:

The factories, particularly in Hung Hom, for women's clothes. Factories, however, may not be well stocked all the time. Four Seasons for silk blouses, shirts and dresses is consistently good, and there are several other factory showrooms in the same area. **Four Seasons** is in Phase II, 1st floor, G1, Kaiser Estate, 51 Man Yuen Street, Hung Hom, Kowloon, (phone 3-632218). Near the airport is **Headline Fashions,** Prince Industrial Bldg., 7/F, 106, King Fuk Street, San Po Kong, Kowloon (phone 3-260225) which has Albert Nippon dresses for about one-third New York prices among its many labels. **Safari** (Central and Jardines Lookout) is good for casual, daytime dresses and men's polo shirts. Many of the factories advertise in the For Sale section of the South China Morning Post's classified advertisements when they have a lot of stock.

The **American Women's Club** regularly updates its list of about 75 factories, all of which have been checked out by members. The products covered are not just clothes, but candles, luggage, jewellery, brassware, porcelain, radio-controlled toy cars, carpets, etc. The AWA is at 48 Kennedy Road, Hong Kong (phone 5-272961). Ask the HKTA about factory visits to see the manufacturing process. Buy also the Hong Kong Guide to Factory Bargains by Dana Goetz.

The **alleys** and **open markets** are also good for bargains: Jardine's Bazaar, Causeway Bay for cheap clothes; Chungking Arcade at 40 Nathan Road, Tsim Sha Tsui for some imported souvenir-type clothes and luggage; the alley between Lock Road and Hankow Road, Tsim Sha Tsui, one block south of Haiphong Road for plastic neksuke, wood carvings and cheap souvenirs; Temple Street Night Market three blocks west of the Jordan Road MTR stop for men's clothing, toys, novelties and handbags; the Macau Ferry

Pier after 7pm; Stanley Market, best for name brand jeans (Jordache, Gloria Vanderbilt, Dior, for about one-third U.S. prices), larger sized clothes, Chinese-made Aran sweaters for one-third Irish prices, porcelain, some arts and crafts, swimming suits, and sneakers in large sizes. See also 'Things to See and Do' for Stanley, page 89.

Millies (Wholesale) outlet in the Peninsula Centre, Tsim Sha Tsui East has everything imaginable: medical instruments, electronics, jewellery, clothes and, despite a profusion of junk, great bargains if you look hard enough and are careful.

What to Buy

Jewellery: For good jewellery, try **Vanessa** in Ocean Terminal, **New Universal** in the Hilton Hotel, or **Dabera** in Swire House, Central. If you are buying expensive gems, it will probably be worth your while to have them tested at one of the gem testing laboratories. These can tell you if a VVS G graded diamond or fancy jade is genuine or fake. The Hong Kong Jewellers and Goldsmiths Association (5-439633), and even some jewellers will test gold content for free.

You could also register with the Diamond Importers Association, Room 401, Hong Kong Diamond Exchange Building, 8-10 Duddell Street, Central (5-235497). You will receive an introduction card to member stores, and maybe discount prices. Hong Kong is the third largest diamond trading centre in the world. You may want to take advantage of this.

Gold: Hong Kong is a good place to buy gold. Note however that gold is 99.99% pure here whereas the international standard is .995. Prices are quoted in taels, one of which is 1.2 troy ounces. King Fook in the Miramar Hotel has a good reputation for gold which is sold at current gold prices. Barter for a 40 per cent discount on its jewellery.

Tailoring: Good Hong Kong tailors no longer do 24-hour jobs. Be sceptical of any that say they can. You should have at least two fittings. Labour costs, still cheaper than in Britain and the U.S., have forced many buyers to look for ready-made clothes. Ultrasuede suits are popular, tailor-made or otherwise. Ask the concierge at your hotel to recommend a tailor as it helps to have an introduction. If you can't find one, try M.K. Loo in the Peninsula Hotel for quality. Also check with Elegante Tailor, 2nd Floor, 8 Hankow Road (3-667352), who will probably send a tailor to your hotel room. Ascot Chang in the Peninsula (3-662398) is a recommended shirt-maker.

Spectacles: Hong Kong is a relatively cheap place to get glasses made, but it is preferable to bring your own prescription. Some stores offer to test eyesight, but their examination may not be reliable.

Cameras: For cameras try Esquire in the Melbourne Plaza on Queen's Road Central (5-233546), or Che Ming (5-768225), or Master Photos

The Peninsula Hotel

(5-7908519). The latter two are behind the Excelsior Hotel in Causeway Bay. But do compare prices and haggle.

Porcelain: For porcelain, try Stanley Market, the China Arts & Crafts stores, and Ah Chow Porcelain Factory, No. 489-491 Castle Peak Road, Hong Kong Industrial Centre, 7th Floor, Block B, Room No. B1 and B2, Lai Chi Kok (3-7451511).

Jade: See Jade market in 'Things to See and Do', page 116. For better jade, try Chow Tai Fook, King Fook, or Jade Creations.

Computers: Golden Shopping Centre, Shamshuipo MTR stop, Kweilin/Fuk Wa Street Exit, Kowloon.

Please note that clothing sizes follow several different systems so check everything you buy for size. A 'medium' tag is not enough. Check shoulder width and length. Hold clothes up to you.

Some stores will ship items for you, or hold them for you while you do further shopping. Hong Kong's postal service is reliable but expensive goods should be insured and registered.

Beware of pirated name-brand goods, which often come complete with 'Made in France' or 'Made in West Germany' labels.

Make sure you have a receipt for expensive purchases with the name of the store, item, brand name and serial and model number if any. For jewellery, there should be a full description, including size of stone, grading (of

diamonds), gold content of setting and return-back policy. Such precautions are for insurance and customs purposes in your own country and are a protection against fakes. It should also mean replacement if purchases are found to be defective.

Check the customs regulations in your own country by telephoning your own consulate if you are buying anything expensive. Ask for example if you can take back elephant ivory or a crocodile leather purse. Dried beef, dried mushrooms and other foodstuffs will probably be seized by U.S. Customs. Find out the rate of duty you may have to pay, your duty-free allowance limit, and how much per parcel you can mail home duty-free.

Bargaining

If you want real bargains, it is best to at least pretend to have an introduction. 'Mrs Fairweather sent me. She said you always give her a good price,' may be all that is necessary. It is also good to go with a trusted local resident. In any case you should always compare prices in several stores. Look for stores with lots of customers (but not a tour group), or be the first customer of the day. Some shopkeepers are superstitious.

The Minolta in one store may be cheaper than in another, but the Pentax may be cheaper in the second. Some stores prefer to quote a discounted price right off and save time. Others will quote first the suggested retail price and then dicker. Prices in large department stores and some smaller stores may be 'fixed' and haggling will be useless.

Haggling should be pleasant and fun. Sample ploys: 'Is that really your best price? I'm not a rich tourist; I live here!' or 'I heard there were some really good buys in Hong Kong but that's the same price as Willoughby's in New York! How about 20 per cent off?' When you have the price as low as you think you can get, then 'How about throwing in a couple rolls of film and a fancy shoulder strap...?' and 'If I take it with me, you'll save delivery charges. How about another $10 off?'

Let the best price and not the size of the discount determine your purchase. Don't haggle with a tailor or a jewellery-maker. If you bargain these down too much, they may try to save money on the thread they use, or the labour, or the gold content of the setting.

Shopping Hours: roughly

Causeway Bay	10 or 11am to 10pm
Central	10am to 6pm
Stanley Market	9.30am to 6.45pm
Tsim Sha Tsui and Mongkok	10am to 10pm
Ocean Terminal and Centre	10am to 7 or 8pm
Tsim Sha Tsui East	10am to 8 or 10pm

Most shops and markets are open for the whole day on Sundays, some only from Sunday noon. Some department stores close one weekday. The only time stores are generally closed is the lunar New Year for two or three days.

Tourist Services

The **Hong Kong Tourist Association** is the most imaginative and aggressive government-sponsored tourist promotion agency in Asia.

Its headquarters is on the 35th Floor, Connaught Centre, Connaught Place, Central, telephone 5-244191. There are smaller offices at the Star Ferry entrance, Tsim Sha Tsui, in the Government Publications Centre, the General Post Office building by the Star Ferry, Hong Kong Island, and in the buffer hall at Kai Tak Airport. During office hours, you can telephone 3-671111 for all kinds of information. The HKTA also has offices in London, Paris, Frankfurt, Rome, New York, Chicago, San Francisco, Tokyo, Osaka, Sydney, Auckland and Singapore. It is represented in other places by Cathay Pacific Airways. These can all help you plan your visit before you come.

A stop to pick up free maps and brochures is imperative early in your visit if you want to plan your time well. Guidance is also available for such activities as sightseeing by public transport, hotels, Chinese festivals, trips to outlying islands, arts and crafts factories and walking tours.

The HKTA can steer you towards guided group tours. Flexible pre-packaged tours with at least three dozen different routes can be booked by a minimum of four people. These tours go on land or sea, day or evening, and range from two hours to two days. Book at a hotel or a travel agent.

For example, a five-hour Arts and Crafts Cooking tour will take you to a temple, a porcelain and jewellery factory and a Chinese cooking demonstration that can be eaten for lunch. A Hong Kong Island Tour will provide you with a mental map of this many-splendoured island: the Peak, Central, Wanchai, Tiger Balm Gardens, Repulse Bay, Deep Water Bay, Aberdeen, the University of Hong Kong, and Western District. If you wish, you can include Stanley and Hollywood Road.

You can cover a lot of these places on your own too, either by public transport or by hiring a car from a hotel with an English-speaking driver. A good hotel concierge can confirm plane bookings for you, obtain visas, Macau ferry and concert tickets, and give you all kinds of advice on what to see.

Hotels

Your choice of overnight accommodation here ranges from top world-class luxury hotels to cheap but clean and adequate dormitories. Until 1982 hotel rooms have been in such short supply that during peak seasons (March-

The lobby of the Shangri-La Hotel

May, September-November) some travellers have had to sleep on chairs at the airport. Those days are probably now over. Not only is it easier to obtain rooms, but during slack seasons some of the top hotels have been giving individual as well as corporate discounts. By the end of 1982 there were 17,911 rooms in 52 hotels. By the end of 1984, 20,000 rooms in 58 hotels are expected to be available. At this rate, discounting in future off-seasons will probably continue, so try for cheaper prices. A reservation during the peak season is still recommended for favourite hotels, however.

The best hotels are the **Regent** and **Peninsula** in Tsim Sha Tsui, the **Shangri-La** in Tsim Sha Tsui East and the **Mandarin** in Central. Next in line and grouped according to location are the **Hilton** and **Furama** in Central, the **Excelsior, Plaza** and **Lee Gardens** in Causeway Bay, the **Holiday Inn Harbour View, Regal Meridien** and **Royal Garden** in Tsim Sha Tsui East; and the **Hongkong, Sheraton, Holiday Inn Golden Mile** and **Hyatt** in Tsim Sha Tsui.

Your choice should take into account location, facilities, and what you want to do in Hong Kong as well as price. Transportation from one area to another is not always easy. The Cross-Harbour Tunnel, which ought to have made Hong Kong Island easily accessible to the airport, is frequently congested. The MTR (subway) has made travelling from one side to the other very fast, but you can't carry heavy luggage on it. The closest hotels to the MTR are the Furama, Mandarin, Hyatt, Holiday Inn Golden Mile and the

Astor; the most distant are the hotels in Causeway Bay (although these are closest to the Cross-Harbour Tunnel). Adjacent to the Star Ferry are the Hongkong and Mandarin hotels. Tsim Sha Tsui East has had severe traffic congestion problems during rush hours although these may be solved in the near future. It is, however, within walking distance (15 minutes) of the Star Ferry and the MTR (10 minutes).

The best tourist shopping area (curios, cameras, electronics) is in Tsim Sha Tsui. Stores in Central close at 6pm, but those in other areas stay open longer. All top hotels have shopping plazas either in or near them.

The main tourist attractions, including the Peak and Aberdeen, are on Hong Kong Island. Top restaurants and bars are ubiquitous, but the liveliest nightlife is in Tsim Sha Tsui. Central is still the prime business district but many firms are escaping high rentals by moving out to Wanchai, Harbour City and Tsim Sha Tsui East. The train station, international ship terminals and the airport are all situated on the Kowloon side. The ferry terminal to Macau is in Central. The best views of Hong Kong harbour are from the Regent, Furama, Excelsior, Mandarin, Shangri-La and Holiday Inn Harbour View hotels. The Regent has a suite with mirrors set in such a way that you feel you're on a ship with water and skyscrapers on both sides. If you want to be near the shops and bright lights but stay on a low budget, try the **YMCA** in Salisbury Road, or **Chungking Mansions** in Tsim Sha Tsui.

All the top hotels have spacious marbled lobbies, several bars and restaurants, and most provide 18- to 20-hour-a-day coffee shops. The Royal Garden has a breathtaking coffee shop with a 13-storey high ceiling. It can also offer two-storey suites with gold-plated bathroom fixtures. All have colour televisions, stocked bars or refrigerators and smoke alarms in rooms. Most have special facilities for business travellers, a 24-hour room service, and either routinely or on request can provide queen or king-sized beds. The Sheraton has a UPI ticker in its lobby.

Many have some kind of exercise facility such as a health centre. Some hotels, such as the Hongkong, Regent, Sheraton, Shangri-La and Hilton have heated outdoor pools usable all year round. The largest swimming pool (2,012 square feet) is at the Regent. The only indoor pool is at the Salisbury Road YMCA. See 'Recreation', page 47 for jogging and other sports.

Top hotels have IDD telephoning from rooms. Many, but not all, have more than one telephone per room, most have a same-day laundry service and in-house movies.

Hong Kong has many cheaper hotels with all the basic amenities, which are clean and well located. Recommended are the **Astor, Empress, Grand, Imperial, International, Marco Polo, New World** and **Park** — all in Tsim Sha Tsui.

Budget travellers should not be apprehensive but should expect a lower standard of English as well as accommodation. Most YMCAs require one day's rent with advance reservations, but if you're lucky you might get a room upon arrival.

Don't be timid about asking to see a hotel room before committing yourself. Hotels are used to this. Harbour views and upper floors usually cost more.

Children

Don't hesitate about bringing children to Hong Kong. Good hotels to stay in are the Excelsior or Plaza, which are both close to spacious parks. The New World and Regent hotels are connected to a small playground by a road overpass. If you stay in the Hong Kong or Marco Polo hotels, the children can wander around the shopping centre without crossing any streets. Budget hostels like the YMCA should help keep down costs. Hamburgers, pizzas, spaghetti and fancy ice-cream sundaes are easily available. So are baby-sitters.

Aside from Chinese opera, more than a few things here should hold the interest of children over six years. Markets where they can see live quail, frogs and turtles are entertainments in themselves except for the sensitive child who may eventually learn where these animals are headed. Children should especially enjoy Ocean Park, Lai Chi Kok, ice skating, ferry and tram rides and the acrobats at the Sung Dynasty Village. There is a small zoo at the Botanical Gardens. Electronic games are available for those who look 16 years or older.

Some Hong Kong Customs

Some Chinese people do have the disgusting habit of spitting on the streets.

Some people, including expatriates, have been arrested and jailed for possession of 'dangerous drugs' such as marijuana.

The system of floor numbers is British. The ground floor is the American or Chinese 'first', the first floor is the 'second' and so on. To be safe, when you are given directions, ask what elevator button to push. Floor references in this guide go by the British system.

Most public toilets here are terrible. Visitors should carry some tissue at all times. Some locals head for a good hotel lavatory (such as the one at the Mandarin Hotel) when nature calls. Residents tip washroom attendants 50 cents to a dollar.

Few people object to having their photograph taken, but your subject will cooperate more readily if you ask first.

Voltage is 220V at 50 Hz.

Sports and Recreation

Hong Kong has some excellent public recreation facilities, but they are often crowded. Use them when most of the population is working or in school, and avoid weekends and holidays.

Alternatively, clubs you belong to may have reciprocal privileges here. Ask your hotel concierge if he can make arrangements for tennis, golf, or whatever.

The Sea Ranch on Lantau Island allows overseas visitors to use its tennis courts, mini-golf, huge swimming pool, wind-surfers, sailing dinghies and spotless beach. Contact Tourist Enterprises Ltd., 54 Cameron Road, Kowloon (3-680647 or 3-689620).

Swimming

Hong Kong is blessed with 41 **public beaches,** all with changing rooms and supervised by lifeguards. Twelve of these are on Hong Kong Island. Most of the time these beaches are clean and beautiful, but occasionally swimmers have to wade through plastic bags and watermelon rinds to enjoy the bathing. Avoid swallowing the water.

Beach on Cheung Chau Island

The closest beaches to the hotels in Causeway Bay, Central and Tsim Sha Tsui are on Hong Kong Island at Repulse Bay, Deep Water Bay and Stanley (buses 6, 260 or 61 from Central, or 63 from Causeway Bay).

Those residents who can afford it hire or buy junks to take them to clean isolated beaches on neighbouring islands. You can do likewise or take a sampan. Check with the Hong Kong Boating Centre (5-223527), or Maition Enterprises (3-311839). Even the Hilton's beautiful brigantine, the 110 ft. *Wan Fu*, can be hired.

You can also reach pleasant beaches by ferry but try to board before 8.15am on hot, sunny, summer Sundays. A 40-minute ride takes you to Sok Kwu Wan on Lamma Island, and a one-hour air-conditioned ferry ride brings you to Silvermine Bay on Lantau. From there, within walking distance or a short bus ride away, you have access to some splendid swimming.

Hong Kong also has some large **outdoor public pools.** The one in Victoria Park, Causeway Bay, is probably the best. The big indoor pool at Chi Fu Fa Yuen (5-506005) on Hong Kong Island is heated.

Scuba diving is available, though many divers find the water too murky as a result of the silt washed down by the Pearl River. Information on diving clubs is available from dive shops such as Bunn's, 188 Wanchai Road, Wanchai (5-721629).

Other water sports abound, some in the most beautiful of settings. **Windsurfing** lessons and rentals are run from Stanley Main Beach (phone Dr or Mrs Howard for information, 5-531115) and the Surf Hotel in Saikung (3-2814411). The Deep Water Bay Speedboat Co. (5-920391) offers waterskiing.

Chartering a yacht without a crew is virtually impossible because a licensed coxswain is required for any ship with a motor. If you want to sail cheaply, contact one of the yacht clubs. The Royal Hong Kong Yacht Club (5-7902817) will post a card in its Course Room with your qualifications, dates in Hong Kong and contact address. Anyone looking for crew will try to reach you. Write to the General Manager, RHKYC, Kellett Island, Causeway Bay, Hong Kong.

One challenging way to spend a few days is to take a course on the Outward Bound brigantine. The *Ji Fung* takes on 40 trainees at a time, and they, along with her seven officers, furl and unfurl her 14 sails on trips to the Philippines or along the China coast. Courses attract families, children and land-weary executives and are reasonably priced. Contact the Outward Bound Trust of Hong Kong, Tai Mong Tsai, Saikung, New Territories (3-2811827).

Fishing licences for the reservoirs can be obtained for a nominal fee from the Waterworks Department in Leighton Centre, Causeway Bay. The season is from September to March.

Jogging

On a clear day the most spectacular course is on the path around the top of the Peak. This involves a 20-minute Peak Tram ride after which you head for Lugard and Harlech roads. A little closer to the hotels in Central is the jog up Garden Road and through the Botanical Gardens, or westward along the waterfront from the City Hall, some of this on breezy, elevated walkways. For the less ambitious, the Hilton Hotel provides free transportation for its guests to uphill starting points.

Hotels in Causeway Bay are close to Victoria Park with its 600-metre jogging trail. The Tsim Sha Tsui hotels are a few fleet steps from Kowloon Park and the 1,200-metre long Kowloon waterfront. Traffic is light until about 8.15am, so start early. The **Hash House Harriers,** a jogging-drinking club popular among expatriates in Asia, organises runs through unlikely places. Write to P.O. Box 20289, Hennessy Road P.O., Wanchai, Hong Kong and hope they will contact you. Alternatively, telephone the **Community Advice Bureau** for the Secretary's telephone number.

Hiking

A labyrinth of paths through Hong Kong's mountainous terrain allows a panoramic perspective of the island-dotted South China Sea and ship-laden Hong Kong harbour. See 'Things to See and Do', page 73.

Tennis

Public tennis courts are open from 7am to 6pm or 11pm. Reservations are necessary. Phone 5-706186 for Victoria Park, 5-749122 for Wongnaichung Road, 3-367878 for Kowloon Tsai Park, or 5-282983 for Bowen Road.

Golf

Golfing can be arranged for non-members on weekdays at the Royal Hong Kong Golf Club. The club has three 18-hole courses in Fanling in the New Territories (0-901211), and nine holes in Deep Water Bay on Hong Kong Island.

Horse Racing

Betting is only legal through the Royal Hong Kong Jockey Club which organises races at the Happy Valley and Shatin racetracks.

Racing here was started shortly after the British took over, as an annual event held over the lunar New Year. The Jockey Club was founded in 1884 with Chinese members first admitted in 1927. In 1960 Queen Elizabeth II

Wind-surfing at Stanley

granted the club its 'Royal' prefix. Professional racing started in 1971 and night racing in 1973. Today, horses are imported from Australia, England, New Zealand, France and Ireland. Jockeys and trainers are of all nationalities.

Races alternate between **Shatin** in the New Territories and **Happy Valley** on Hong Kong Island near Causeway Bay. The newer Shatin track was built in 1978, and has a 700-ft. long grandstand, mostly air-conditioned, accommodating 30,900 racegoers. A totalizator system gives immediate information on odds, and one of the biggest video matrix screens in the world relays a close-up of the action complete with an instant replay and slow-motion sequences. Happy Valley also has two tracks. Its grandstand holds 52,000.

From September to the end of May races take place every Saturday and some Sundays from 1 to 6pm. Night races are mostly on Wednesdays but sometimes on Tuesdays from 7.15 to 10.30.

The best way to reach Shatin is by electric train; it takes about 10 minutes from Hung Hom station. Bumper to bumper road traffic may make the trip over an hour. Visitor's badges can be obtained from some of the RHKJC betting centres and you will have to show your passport to get into the members' enclosure. For information, call 5-7906321. Don't feel too bad if you lose money. The Jockey Club donates about HK$252,696,000 a year to

View from the Peak, with Lamma Island in the background

worthwhile community projects such as sports facilities, hospitals, clinics and parks.

Keeping Fit

Tai Chi Chuan is the Chinese way of keeping fit, and you can see practitioners out at dawn in parks and by the waterfront, going through the slow, dream-like motions that actually tax more muscles than many other sports. You may find some adherents happy to give you a spontaneous lesson. Regular classes are held at Chater Garden in Central, Victoria Park in Causeway Bay, and in Kowloon Park. Times: 7.30am, Monday to Friday, October to February. Contact Recreation and Sports Service, Central Office (5-438559) for further details.

Ice Skating

The newest and best maintained rink is at Cityplaza, Taikoo Shing (5-675388). Easier to get to from the MTR and with a larger skating area is the rink at Lai Chi Kok amusement park (Lai Wan MTR stop). Skates are available for hire.

Arts and Entertainment

Hong Kong has much to offer patrons of the arts, and those who don't expect London, New York or Beijing standards are pleasantly surprised. It has its own good 82-piece philharmonic orchestra, a 75-piece Chinese orchestra, a professional Chinese repertory theatre, innumerable professional Cantonese opera troupes, several English and Chinese-language amateur theatre companies and amateur dance groups.

None are good enough to warrant a special trip here but they are nevertheless worth seeing. You may however want to plan a trip around a concert by some of the high calibre international artists who occasionally perform in Hong Kong. These have included Vladimir Ashkenazy, Maxim Shostakovich, the Royal Ballet, Helen Reddy, Sarah Vaughan, the Clash and the Boomtown Rats.

The **Festival of Asian Arts** is usually held in the autumn and lasts for two weeks. It brings together some of Asia's best dance companies, choral groups, orchestras and operas and incorporates the traditional with the modern. The month-long **Hong Kong Arts Festival** in February presents mainly western music, theatre, mime and dance, and some Chinese arts as well.

Tickets for outstanding performers are usually snapped up months in advance. It is not easy for visitors to get tickets without a willing locally-based friend or travel agent to help. You could write for a copy of the relevant programme and booking folder from the Urban Council, GPO Box 10688, Hong Kong (5-268673). Tickets are sometimes returned to the box office at the last moment or a well-connected hotel concierge or assistant manager may be able to help you. Lists of current performances and exhibitions are published in the local newspapers and in the various 'What's On' giveaways usually found in hotels.

The **Hong Kong Tourist Association** presents free cultural performances in the open space in the first-floor link between **Ocean Centre** and **Ocean Terminal** in Tsim Sha Tsui. The Wednesday 6pm performances include Chinese puppets, dances, instrumental music, acrobats and martial arts displays. Free performances are also held on Sunday afternoons in the **Landmark** in Central.

The usual venues for cultural performances are the **City Hall** in Central by the Star Ferry (5-229928 or 5-229511), or within the intimate auditoria of the **Arts Centre** in Wanchai (5-280626), at the corner of Harbour Road and Fenwick Street by the waterfront. The **Academic Community Hall** of Baptist College, 224 Waterloo Road, Kowloon (3-386121), and **Queen Elizabeth Stadium** on Queen's Road East in Wanchai (5-756793) are also widely used.

Three or four times a year, the **Hilton Hotel** has a dinner theatre, usually a comedy from London's West End. Some of the top hotels and night clubs also import big international names.

Movies

These are mostly British, U.S., Hong Kong or China-made. They usually run on a schedule of 12.30, 2.30, 5.30, 7.30 and 9.30pm showings. Consequently, long films are often butchered to fit the schedule, but the censor also has a sharp pair of scissors. All seats are numbered and reserved and tickets can be bought one or two days in advance, a wise move if the movie is new and popular. Most cinemas are divided into 'dress circle' or 'deluxe' seats, and the cheaper front and back stalls. Some theatres are adjacent and a few patrons have made the mistake of buying seats for the wrong one. Most good Chinese movies are in Cantonese with English subtitles, while western films are shown in English with Chinese subtitles.

China-made movies are usually shown at the Astor and Nanyang theatres.

Television

About 98 per cent of Hong Kong's households have television sets. There are four channels, two in English and two in Cantonese. Some hotels have in-house movies.

Paintings

The City Hall in Central (5-224127) has good and changing exhibitions of ceramics, traditional Chinese paintings and paintings of historical interest. Occasionally the Chinese University in Shatin, New Territories (0-633111) has some excellent art exhibits, primarily for its own students but open also to the public.

Museums

If you like museums, Hong Kong's best are small but of sure merit. The **Museum of History** (3-671124) is situated in Blocks 61 and 62, Kowloon Park. Enter by Haiphong Road entrance. It might host anything from an exhibit of local fishing boats, photos of old Hong Kong or a project about pre-British times. Archaeological books and maps are available for sale.

The **Fung Ping Shan Museum** at Hong Kong University, 94 Bonham Road, Hong Kong Island (5-468161), has a good collection of bronzes from the Shang dynasty, and 966 Nestorian crosses dating from Yuan times (1271-1368 A.D.). The museum also has ancient ceramics, paintings and sculptures on display.

Lei Cheng Uk Branch Museum encompasses a tomb believed to be from the Later Han period (25-220 A.D.). It is the oldest structure so far found in Hong Kong. A visit is only of interest to the serious archaeologist as the tomb is like a small kiln and there are only a few clay figures on display. It is situated at 41 Tonkin Street, Lei Cheng Uk Resettlement Estate, Sham Shui Po, Kowloon, ten minutes walk northeast along Tonkin Street from the Cheung Sha Wan MTR station (3-862863).

Commercial Exhibitions

From time to time commercial exhibitions of special crafts, jewellery and antiques are held. Some of these are organised by Chinese government agencies. Others, like the reputable International Asian Antiques Fair in May, are privately run. Here even non-buyers are welcome to inspect such antique wares as Three-Colour Tang pottery (produced between the 7th and 10th centuries A.D.), or even Zhou bronzes (7th-6th centuries B.C.).

Chinese Opera

One has to learn about Chinese opera to appreciate it. The acrobatic fight scenes are dramatically executed and the costumes beautiful but that is all most foreigners can enjoy. Performers sing in screaming falsetto voices, plots seem interminable and scenery is sparse.

The stylised gestures and expressions of Chinese opera

A Chinese opera fan will know the plot beforehand and take a heightened pleasure from the quality of the stylised singing and acting. A well-performed tremble of anguish by the hero, or a graceful pantomine as the 'young girl' feeds chickens will result in sighs of appreciation from devotees. Plots are usually drawn from Chinese mythology and history, conflicts between love and duty, or from literature such as the war stories based on the classic novel, *The Romance of the Three Kingdoms*. Overt expressions of affection are forbidden but fight scenes are mandatory. Make-up is used literally to 'paint in' the audience's knowledge of the various characters.

The best troupes are from China and Taiwan, but Hong Kong is developing its own indigenous theatre. Look for opera performances on television and then decide if you want to spend an evening watching it live. Phone the HKTA and ask if any is currently being shown.

Nightlife

Hong Kong offers a wide choice of good night spots in which to relax or unwind, the setting either exotic or familiar. The town livens up on Friday and Saturday nights, and before a holiday. At such times the prices are higher and the hours longer. Reservations are recommended for discos and dinner.

Pubs and some hotel bars are packed from 6 to 8pm as locals relax before dinner. Many bars have 'Happy Hours' with drinks at half price, or with free 'small chow' or snacks. Business is quiet during dinnertime, but starts moving again around 10.30 and 11pm especially when there is a fleet in port.

The popular brews are San Miguel, Carlsberg and Heineken but others are available. Hong Kong's own cocktail is the Cheong Sam, named after the high-necked, high-slit, traditional Chinese dress. The ingredients are gin, white creme-de-menthe, maraschino, fresh lemon juice, Seven-Up, egg white, cherry, lemon and cucumber slices, and mint.

The minimum age for bars is 18 but the ruling is not strictly enforced. Pay your bills with a credit card only in reputable establishments. Some bars have been known to run a card through the machine twice, forging your signature on the second chit. Discos charge an entrance fee which includes two standard drinks.

If so inclined, you can go into a 'girlie bar', ignore the girls and still get a cheap drink. These bars make their money when you buy a girl a drink at some wildly inflated price. Girls might stay with you for about 15 minutes per drink. Don't be timid about asking the prices and paying as each glass arrives. Some bars will allow their girls to be 'bought out' for escort service. This is usually cheaper than hiring a date from an escort service or going to a hostess club.

The following night spots are the favourites of some local foreign residents. They are listed according to location and you can walk from one to the other within each group. Taxis are easily hailed after the evening rush hour and tend to cruise the bright-light districts. Bear in mind that the last Star ferry is at 11.30pm and the last MTR leaves just before 1am. After that you can get from one side of the harbour to the other through the tunnel by taking an all-night bus or by taxi.

The price of a San Miguel beer ('San Mig') is listed only to give an idea of its comparative cost.

Central

The **Bull and Bear,** Hutchison House, next to the Furama Hotel (phone 5-257436). 11.30am to 1.30am. Strictly an English pub with oak beams, Tudor maids, and dart boards. Steak and kidney pie and toasted sandwiches are the staple fare. San Mig HK$6.

Lau Ling Bar, Furama Hotel (phone 5-255111). Decor is Chinese. Happy hour with free *dim sum* snack from 5.30pm to 7.30pm. Live entertainment from 6pm to 1am. San Mig HK$10. Minimum charge at weekends.

The **Godown,** basement, Sutherland House (next to the Furama Hotel) at 3 Chater Road (phone 5-221608). Noon to 3pm and 7pm to 2am. Good choice for a medium-priced dinner too. On Wednesdays from 9.30pm to midnight there is a good jazz band performing. On other nights there is dancing after 10pm. Darts and backgammon. Rustic atmosphere. San Mig HK$5.50.

Dragonboat Bar, Hilton Hotel (phone 5-233111). 11am to 1am. Dutifully oriental with lanterns and a genuine dragonboat. San Mig HK$9.

Disco Disco, 40 D'Aguilar Street (phone 5-235863). Hours fluctuate according to the day of the week. On Sundays and Tuesdays only teenagers and soft-drinks permitted, 7.30pm to midnight. On Mondays, only people connected with the entertainment business are allowed entry. Don't be discouraged however, and check if they have a policy change these days. This is one of Hong Kong's most popular discos. All mirrors, flashing lights and mystifying smoke. It lays claim to the largest dance floor in town and the latest music from the U.S. and Europe. This institution has a reputation locally for being a gay hangout but 'straights' seem to be in the vast majority. Prices are reasonable. No reservations. Very crowded at weekends.

Wanchai

Old China Hand, 104 Lockhart Road (phone 5-279174). Noon to 2am. Small pub with its own clique of loyal regulars, English food and two dartboards. San Mig HK$7.

The **Front Page,** 3rd Floor, 175 Lockhart Road (phone 5-752623). 11am to 2am. Old World decor, Happy Hour from 5 to 8pm. Sometimes a singer and band on Fridays and Saturdays from 8 to 11pm. Rock dancing from 11pm to 1am. Favourite of trendy set. Good, medium-priced western food. San Mig HK$11.

Hong Kong night scene

Makati Inn, 18 Luard Road, 1st Floor (phone 5-270117). 4pm to 5am.
Tacky disco and bar, a local hangout for Filipinos who generate a friendly
atmosphere. At the weekends, lots of single women customers who might be
persuaded to dance. Happy Hour 4pm to 9pm with 30 per cent discount on
drinks. Dancing from 8pm and live music from 10pm. San Mig HK$10.

Dickens Bar, Excelsior Hotel (phone 5-767365). 11am to 2am, later on
Saturdays. British pub. Live entertainment from 9pm to 1.30am. Jazz from
3pm to 6pm every Sunday. San Mig HK$5.

Talk of the Town, 34th Floor, Excelsior Hotel (phone 5-767365).
Lounge and disco. Excellent view of harbour. The 'no jeans or rubber shoes'
ruling indicates an older crowd. Happy Hour from 4.30 to 8.30pm (San Mig
costing HK$8). From 9pm a medium-priced admission charge for dancing.
Live band alternates with a disc-jockey.

Club Dai-Ichi, 1st Floor, Harbour View Mansion, 257 Gloucester Road
(phone 5-768991). 2pm to 4am. Happy Hour until 9pm reduces drinks to
about half-price. San Mig HK$10. Try this only if you want to experience a
hostess club. This one is big, expensive and elegant. Floor show. Hostesses.
Mostly Chinese and Japanese clientele. Entrance fee. Private VIP rooms.
Hostesses here can be 'bought out'. Only male customers welcome.

Tsim Sha Tsui

Chin Chin Bar, Hyatt Regency Hotel (3-662321). 11 to 2am. Happy Hour before 9pm means *dim sum* snacks and San Mig at HK$9 (HK$12 later). Two singers after 5.30pm. Classy Chinese decor.

Bottoms Up, 14-16 Hankow Road (phone 3-663336). 5pm to 3am. Happy Hour before 9pm, HK$12.50 instead of HK$18.50 for a San Mig. Shapely, topless barmaids. Relaxing atmosphere with amicable manager, Pat Sephton, a former Windmill Theatre showgirl. Four mirror-enclosed rooms. Occasional impromptu late-night jam sessions. Hostess drinks cost HK$25. This bar was the setting for a scene in the movie *Man with the Golden Gun.*

Ned Kelly's Last Stand, 11A Ashley Road (phone 3-660562). 11.30pm to 2.15am. Happy Hour to 7pm, HK$4.50 instead of HK$7 for San Mig. Seven-man jazz band daily (except Wednesdays) from 9pm to 2am considered the best in town. Bangers-and-mash, meat pies and steaks available. Rustic Australian decor. No minimum or cover.

Red Lips Bar, 1A Lock Road (3-684511). 10.30am to 3 or 4am. This tiny, shabby bar where the bar-maids are none too young is nevertheless highly recommended by locals — usually with a grin. It is reminiscent of the bars of the Vietnam era, not just here but all over Asia. A San Mig costs HK$5, a drink for a hostess HK$11.

Bar City, second basement level, New World Centre, 20 Salisbury Road (3-698571). 9pm to 2 or 3am. Complex of six different bars. You can buy discount tickets which will allow you one drink in each bar. A favourite with Americans is the **Country and Western Bar** with horse, appropriate music and a floor strewn with peanut shells. The **Suzie Wong Bar** is appointed in a classy Chinese style with overhead fans and two strip shows. **Mingles** is a singles disco frequented mainly by teenagers. No hostesses. Live entertainment. Beer prices vary according to bar.

Hollywood East Disco, Hotel Regal Meridien, Tsim Sha Tsui East (3-7225597). 9pm to 2 or 3am. Models, actors, actresses and airline hostesses allowed in free. The more outrageous the dress the better. Thirty-six projectors flash mood-setting Hollywood stills. Hot dogs available. Expensive entrance fee.

Festivals

Hong Kong's festivals are colourful affairs, some of which urge the visitor to participate in full. If you want to get a lot of sightseeing, shopping or business done, avoid the lunar New Year. Everything closes down for at least three days. Those places that do remain open are jammed. Public transport continues on a holiday schedule.

Chinese festivals follow the lunar calendar, and so the **lunar New Year** celebrations are at the end of January or early February. This is a time for new beginnings. No one wants to start the year bad-tempered, in debt, or with old clothes. Buildings and boats are spruced up and decorated with flags and representations of the new year's animal. This might be a rabbit, horse, monkey or any of a cycle of twelve. Peach and plum blossoms and kumquat plants, their fruit like tiny balls of gold, brighten up every home. Brooms are hidden; nobody wants to sweep away good luck. Every baby has a birthday.

Visits are paid to members of the family and friends who may have been neglected most of the year (even if they live in China). All transportation is booked up as at least a quarter of a million people carry presents to relatives in the motherland. Others head elsewhere. Children, servants and younger siblings receive lucky money, or *laisee*, from their seniors. *Laisee* is given in small red and gold envelopes which are available free from banks should you likewise want to distribute some. It is always comprised of crisp new bills.

Some play mah-jong all night or go to Macau to try their luck, and even those who do not normally gamble are tempted. Fortunes are read. Temples are crowded with worshippers. Spring fairs swirl in Victoria Park on Hong Kong Island. While officially the holiday is three days long, it may take about two weeks before life returns to normal. Traditionally the festival is concluded with the lantern festival on the 15th day.

The Mid-Autumn Festival coincides with the full harvest moon, the most beautiful of the year. Many people burn candles in brightly-coloured lanterns made in the shape of all kinds of animals, aeroplanes and ships, before going out to enjoy the moon, especially in Victoria Park in Causeway Bay where there is a lantern competition.

Moon cakes are reminiscent of the time when anti-Mongol forces passed messages concealed inside such cakes. They are made of ground lotus, sesame seeds or dates. The best ones have an unbroken duck egg yolk, like a full moon, inside.

Ching Ming, in early April, is more of a festival to watch. At this time graves are cleaned and food shared with ancestors who are believed to influence the fortunes of the living. Families cart whole barbecued suckling pigs, cooked chickens, fruit and buns to cemeteries. There they share the essence of the food with the deceased, pouring out favourite wines and burning incense in front of gravestones. Worshippers bow their heads three times in respect and gratitude. Paper money, usually colourful notes drawn on the Bank of Hell, is burned for use in the afterlife. A similar grave-sweeping festival takes place in October.

During the **Chung Yeung,** many people also climb mountains, a practice based on the story of a man who took his family to a high place upon the advice of a fortune-teller. Upon his return he found that everyone in his home village had been killed.

The **Tin Hau Festival** in May celebrates the birthday of the Queen of Heaven, the patron saint of fisherfolk. This sees boats bedecked with brightly coloured flags and red, plastic windmills (to blow away bad luck and to blow in good fortune). Queues of worshippers, eyes smarting from incense smoke, pay respect at any of more than 20 temples, especially at the oldest and most famous in Joss House Bay in Saikung, New Territories. Elaborately decorated tablets about three metres high are brought to be blessed and the statue of Tin Hau is paraded around. No boat leaves without turning three large circles to ensure the goddess won't think her worshippers are in a hurry to leave. The **Tam Kung Festival** honours another patron saint of boat people and is held in Shaukeiwan also during May. Lion dances are confined to boats because rival groups of dancers tend to become very pugnacious.

The **Bun Festival** is peculiar to Cheung Chau Island. It is held in May to appease the spirits of people tortured and murdered by pirates. The festival continues for about five days with Cantonese opera and lion dances. Then on Sunday, the most spectacular day for tourists, children about four years old, dressed as good and bad spirits, are paraded through the streets and pathways as if they were floating on air. Three 20-metre high towers covered with buns are offered to the gods. On the next day five or six village officials climb the towers and bring down the bean-filled buns. These are distributed at the temple for medicinal purposes.

Bright colourful costumes are a feature of Hong Kong's many festivals.

Birthday celebrations for the Buddha are best seen at Po Lin Monastery on Lantau Island, towards the end of May. See 'Things to See and Do', page 73

The **Dragon Boat Festival** is held in June and commemorates the suicide by drowning in 277 B.C. of Chu Yuan. This poet-statesman was protesting against corrupt government. The boat races symbolise the attempt to save him, and to keep fish from eating his body by distracting them with a special dumpling. Drums pound and paddles beat the water for the same reason. The narrow boats, 45 to 120 feet long, are fashioned with dragons' heads and tails. Like the Tin Hau Festival, the principal celebrants are boat people.

Local races are held in such fishing communities as Stanley, Saikung, Aberdeen and Yau Ma Tei. International dragon boat races are organized by the HKTA and held in Hong Kong harbour. Tickets are available from HKTA offices. Teams come from Singapore, Penang, Macau and, on occasion, from the UK, Australia and Japan.

During **Yue Lan,** the Festival of the Hungry Ghosts in August, you will see small bonfires on the streets, smoking incense and plates of food being offered to keep itinerant spirits happy.

Food and Drink

Hong Kong can serve up some of the best Chinese food in the world and a Chinese banquet should be included in your programme. Since Hong Kong is predominantly Cantonese, it is especially important for you to try at least one Cantonese meal. As top cooks are constantly being seduced from one restaurant to another, we can only recommend the eating houses of long-standing repute.

Generally speaking, Chinese food is best eaten in groups of four to twelve, the more the better. Ideally a knowledgeable local person ought to order but novices can usually trust a waiter to make suggestions. Ensure you know how much each dish will cost before you make your choice. Singles and small groups won't starve but there will not be as much variety.

Chinese food is exciting because of the great variety of tastes and textures — something for everybody, pleasant surprises, crisp vegetables, tender fish slices that melt in your mouth, and as many as five or six ingredients in one course. You will find things you may not recognise. Only eat and enjoy. Trust the experience of 4,000 years of discriminating culinary history.

Many restaurants are used to dealing with patrons who know little or nothing about Chinese food. Menus are usually in English and Chinese. Order as many courses as there are people at the table, plus rice or noodles. Vary the ingredients — one fish course, one pork, one poultry, one beef, one vegetable dish. Vary the manner of cooking — one stir-fry, one steamed, one deep-fried, one roasted, one soup, etc. And vary the seasonings — one sweet and sour, one salty, one peppery hot, one with nuts, etc. If you have more than five people, start again. Dishes are shared by everyone at the table. If you can't use chopsticks, ask for a fork and spoon.

A glossy look to a restaurant does not mean the food is good. Everything depends on the cook. Reservations are recommended for popular restaurants during busy periods such as holidays, Sundays and lunchtimes (usually 1 to 2pm). Some restaurants, especially those of the *dim sum* type, will not accept reservations so try to arrive by noon. Dinnertime is usually 7.30 to 9pm.

A top-class restaurant will have waiters serving you in private banquet rooms, changing your plates and bringing towels at every opportunity. Vegetables cut in the shape of animals and flowers will decorate every course, and only one course will be available at a time.

In most restaurants, however, you will have to serve yourself. You could politely break into each new course by serving the people beside you first. Several courses will be on your table at the same time and, if the table is large enough, these dishes can be passed around. Otherwise, it is customary to reach family-style into the middle, your chopsticks lending an extra few inches to your arm.

Frequent toasting is mandatory if you are in Chinese company. Chinese people do not like to drink alone. Soft drinks, beer and Chinese liquors can usually be ordered. Most restaurants do not object if you bring your own bottle.

In spite of generally high standards of hygiene, upset stomachs do sometimes occur. Especially in hot weather, avoid raw fish, small fish and shellfish. Don't eat anything raw unless peeled, cooked or from America, as the Chinese use nightsoil for fertiliser. It is safe to drink the water although the taste of chlorine is rather strong. High class restaurants use bottled water which is more palatable.

Seafood

The best is of course the freshest, and Hong Kong's 5,000 fishing boats and 44,000 acres of fish farms supply most of the fish eaten here. The freshest fish will be alive on arrival at the restaurant. Pick the liveliest and have it killed on the spot. Shrimps, lobsters and some fish are sold by the 'catty' (1.33 pounds or .604 kg). One and a half catty of steamed shrimp is sufficient for four people if you are having other dishes too.

A good seafood restaurant is **Fook Lam Moon,** 459 Lockhart Road, Wanchai (5-762260) or 31 Mody Road, Tsim Sha Tsui (3-688755). Some of the best seafoods are available in less salubrious surroundings. See 'Adventurous Eating', page 72.

Even chefs in large hotels still use the traditional wok

Dim Sum

Dim sum, known also as *Yum Cha*, is another Hong Kong speciality; savouring them is an experience not to be missed. A seemingly infinite variety of food will be brought to the table on trolleys. You can choose what looks most appetising. A knowledge of Chinese is usually unnecessary. Your waiter will ask what kind of tea you want and then leave you to the women with the trolleys who sing out their wares. After you have finished, your waiter will count your plates and bamboo baskets and let you know the total costs. It usually isn't very much unless you have chosen the crispy pork or roast duck.

Because *dim sum* is such a popular lunchtime custom, try to get to the restaurant before 12.15 — but not much before; the best offerings are served from then until 1.15, after which they are no longer hot and freshly cooked. You might try the **Oceania** Restaurant on the top floor of the Ocean Terminal (3-670181), or the **Blue Heaven** at 38 Queen's Road Central (5-24300l). For a quieter atmosphere without the trolleys, make a reservation at the **Rainbow Room** of the Lee Gardens Hotel in Causeway Bay (5-7954690).

Recommended Cantonese Restaurants:

King Bun, 158 Queen's Road C.(5-434256), a favourite with local Chinese.

Shang Palace, Shangri-La Hotel, Tsim Sha Tsui (3-7212111). Very expensive but worth it.

Eagle's Nest, Hilton Hotel, Central (5-233111). Other regional Chinese dishes are also available. Ballroom dancing. Open 7.30pm.

Jade Garden, Connaught Centre, Central (5-238811).

Luk Yu Tea House, 26 Stanley Street, Central (5-235464). *Dim sum* is tops here but it's hard to get a lunchtime reservation.

For medium prices, try:

Tai Ping Koon Restaurant, 6 Pak Sha Road (behind the Lee Gardens Hotel), Causeway Bay (5-769161). Very popular with local Chinese. Austere-looking. Rice birds a specialty in September-October. Pigeons.

Orchid Garden, 37 Hankow Road, Tsim Sha Tsui (3-7210030), or 481 Lockhart Road, Causeway Bay (5-777151).

Regional Cuisines

Chiu Chow

Chiu Chow food is a variation of Cantonese cuisine. A strong tea, *Teek Goon Yum,* is served before and after meals to increase the appetite and help digestion. As well as the *dim sum,* try the Soyed Goose, Boiled Beef with Satay Sauce, Bean Sprouts, Steamed Crab Claws and Chiu Chow Shark's Fin Soup. Recommended is the **Chiu Chow Garden Restaurant,** Hennessy Centre, 2F & 3F, Causeway Bay (5-773391 or 5-762833).

Peking

Peking cooking makes use of some strong flavours, especially garlic, relying on noodles and dumplings, and not rice, as a base. Dishes have fewer sauces than Cantonese. Exotic dishes include Peking Duck (the meat being wrapped in a thin pancake along with green onion and hoisin sauce) and Beggar's Chicken (which is baked in mud). Both of these are specialities at the **Peking Garden** in Alexandra House, between the Landmark and Swire House (5-266456), and in the Excelsior Hotel arcade in Causeway Bay (5-777231). An entertaining demonstration of noodle-making by hand is given at 8.30pm daily.

Also for the gourmand are the **American Restaurant,** 20 Lockhart Road, Wanchai (5-277770), and the Spring Deer, 42 Mody Road, Tsim Sha Tsui (3-664012).

Some of these Peking restaurants also serve Shanghainese food. Try Sautéd Shrimps and Crispy Rice in Tomato Sauce, Drunken Chicken or Crab, Stewed Turtle, Snow-white Crab in Shell, and Fried Crisp Duck.

Szechuan

Szechuan cooking is noted for its hot chilli peppers, but not all of it is highly spiced. Check the spice level with the waiter first as it can easily be toned up or down. Alternatively, the heat can be cooled off with rice or cucumbers. The food can also be rather oily, and is served with either rice, noodles or dumplings. Favourite dishes are Hot-Sour Soup (vinegary), Spiced Fried Prawn, and Smoked Tea-flavoured Duck.

Recommended are the **Red Pepper,** 7 Lan Fong Road, directly behind the Lee Gardens Hotel, Causeway Bay (5-768046 or 5-773811); **Pep 'N Chili,** 12 Blue Pool Road, Shop F, Happy Valley, Hong Kong (5-738251); **Szechuan Lau,** 466 Lockhart Road, Wanchai (5-7902571), or the **Kam Kong Chuen** Restaurant, 60A Granville Road, Tsim Sha Tsui (3-673434).

Vegetarian

Buddhist restaurants give a good imitation of meat, mainly with soybeans, mushrooms and bamboo shoots. Some of these dishes are quite successful but a lot of monosodium glutamate seems to be added. People sensitive to this 'flavour' intensifier should avoid this kind of cooking or tell the cook not to put it in. In Chinese it is called *mei ding.* A recommended vegetarian restaurant is the **Wishful Cottage,** 336-340 Lockhart Road, Wanchai (5-735645).

Desserts and Drinks

Chinese meals go light on sweet desserts. Who has room? Traditionally, fresh fruit is served and fresh oranges are believed to temper the effects of liquor. Try regional fruits such as lychees, long an, pomelo, pineapple, sweet tiny bananas, mangoes, Hami melon and Tientsin pears.

Some traditional sweets are available. A favourite of foreign visitors is apple or banana fritters in sugar syrup, caramelised by dipping into ice water at the table.

Jasmine *(heung peen)* tea is a favourite of foreigners, but *Po Lay* is better for you with fried foods in hot weather. Oolong tea is a good all-round drink.

Hong Kongers may prefer French brandy, Remy Martin or Courvoisier with meals. If you want to be exotically Chinese, a yellow wine is a fine complement, especially when served hot in the wintertime. Mao tai is the very potent liquor popular in mainland China.

If you are still uncertain about trying Chinese food on your own, the HKTA has an excellent booklet on how to order and eat Chinese food. Otherwise you might invite a knowledgeable person along, or ask the hotel concierge if he knows of someone who can join you.

Food From Other Countries

The Hong Kong eating adventure includes foods from other countries as well. Phone for reservations and information, especially about jacket and tie.

American Food: Beverly Hills Deli, L2-55 New World Centre, Salisbury Road, Tsim Sha Tsui (3-698695).

American and Anzac Steaks: Dairy Farm Steakery, Beach Road, Repulse Bay (5-920360) is medium priced. The Palm Restaurant, 38 Lock Road, Tsim Sha Tsui (3-7211271) and The Steak House, Regent Hotel, Tsim Sha Tsui (3-7211211) are justifiably expensive.

European Food: La Plume, Regent Hotel, Tsim Sha Tsui (3-7211211). Gaddi's, Peninsula Hotel, Tsim Sha Tsui (3-666251). Margaux, Shangri-La Hotel, Tsim Sha Tsui East (3-7212111). Cafe d'Amigo, 79A Wongnaichung Road, Happy Valley (5-772202).

Less expensive European Food: Au Trou Normand, 6 Carnarvon Road, Tsim Sha Tsui (3-668754). Delicatessen Corner (for German food), Holiday Inn Golden Mile, Tsim Sha Tsui (3-693111). Alexander Restaurant, 1 Lan Fong Road (behind the Lee Gardens Hotel), Causeway Bay (5-764465). Paprika (for Hungarian dishes), Ocean Centre, Tsim Sha Tsui (3-690806).

Indian: Ashoka, 57 Wyndham Street, Central (5-255719). Gaylord, 43 Chatham Road, Tsim Sha Tsui (3-675039).

Japanese: All Japanese restaurants are expensive. One of the best is the Benkay in the basement of the Landmark in Central. It contains a *sushi* bar and serves excellent *sashimi* and *tempura* (5-213344). Consider also Shiki in the Furama Hotel, Central (5-264605) and at 20 Queen's Road Central (5-254182). Both specialise in *teppanyaki*. Yagyu Restaurant, 13-17 Stanley Street, Central (5-239529) is less expensive.

Korean: Gogujang Korean Restaurant, Lee Gardens Hotel, Causeway Bay (5-7954690). Korea House Restaurant, Empire Centre, Tsim Sha Tsui East (3-678607).

Vietnamese: Perfume River, 51 Hennessy Road, Wanchai (5-278644). Vietnamese Restaurant, 3A Wyndham Street, Central (5-225523).

A mixed menu of different Asian dishes and a good view of the harbour can be found at the medium-priced Spice Market, Hongkong Hotel, 2nd Floor, Ocean Terminal entrance, Tsim Sha Tsui (3-676238).

Buffets

Usually available only at lunchtime, these are a good way to sample Chinese food. Usually a mixture of several styles. Get there early, no later than 12.15 when the food is just put out and the vegetables crisp. These are not cheap. Most hotels have one, a favourite being **La Ronda** at the Furama in Central (5-255111) because of its revolving restaurant and wide selection. Another good buffet is the **Coffee Garden** at the Shangri-La in Tsim Sha Tsui (3-7212111). Among the cheapest is the Hongkong Hotel's **Spice Market** in Tsim Sha Tsui (3-676238).

Budget Eating

If you're saving your money to shop or eating just to survive, look for a clean, outdoor alley restaurant serving noodles, *dim sum* or congee. Some of these can be good, but the standards are below those of Singapore. If you're worried about cleanliness do as the natives do and sterilise your dishes and chopsticks with hot tea.

You can get sandwiches or Chinese food in lunch boxes at **Maxim's** fast food shops and other snack bars.

Adventurous Eating

The eating of any new food is an adventure, even more so if the meal is served up in an open-air, dumpy seafood restaurant or on a sampan. Those choosing the latter may find the table cover to be a newspaper, and your garbage dumped with it into the waters of the typhoon shelter even before you leave. If this thought is repulsive to you, then you might best forgo this section. But visitors intent on eating somewhere unusual have found Lei Yue Mun, Lamma Island, Po Toi Island and the Causeway Bay Typhoon Shelter delightful.

Some people may want to take their own chopsticks. You can always scald your plates and bowls with hot tea and wash that overboard. The best time is after dark, with the garbage in the water out of sight and mind.

Lei Yue Mun is reached by taxi after going to Kwun Tong at the end of the MTR line. It can also be reached by ferry from Shaukeiwan pier and a short sampan ride to the restaurants. There you pick your fish and insist on it being killed on the spot. The merchant will tell you which restaurant to go to.

At the Causeway Bay **Typhoon Shelter,** you rent a sampan by the hour. The price is less than HK$100 for the boat depending on how well you haggle. You are then paddled out to the biggest of the floating kitchens where you order your food. A floating band with accompanying bar will come to your boat and, for a fee, perform. Afterwards, many people walk over to the nearby Excelsior Hotel for dessert.

Po Toi and So Ku Wan are both on islands, best reached by hiring a boat. They are also accessible by public ferry from the Outlying Districts Ferry pier to the right of the Star Ferry in Central. **Sok Ku Wan** on Lamma is closer and has more frequent ferry services from both Central and Aberdeen, but **Po Toi** is a tinier community on a smaller, more isolated island. If you wish you can combine a trip to Po Toi with a look at some barely discernible rock carvings believed to have been etched between 1200 and 400 B.C. These are behind the chicken-wire barrier evident between the village and the beach. If you climb the hills on Po Toi, you can see nearby Chinese islands. To go to the best of the restaurants, turn right from the ferry pier and just before the second bridge, and the edge of town, turn right again.

At Sok Ku Wan, try Sum Kee to the right of the ferry pier and along the waterfront. It is open from 11am to about 11pm. Telephone 9820241.

Many of these islands have fish farms in their harbours frequently guarded by dogs. Lamma is five square miles and the third largest island. Many archaeological artifacts have been found on it.

Chinese Cooking

Demonstrations are held twice a week at the Town Gas Centre in Leighton Centre in Causeway Bay. Telephone 5-761535 for times and just drop in. Even if you're not interested in learning Lucy Lo's recipes, she is a joy to watch as she stirs sauces with her fingers, pirouettes around her wok and, best of all, gives all her pupils a sample.

Things to See and Do

If you want a comprehensive Hong Kong experience, here are some guidelines. You may, however, decide you would do better with a packaged group tour because of the problems of transport. Another possibility, particularly if you are four or five people, is to hire a car by the hour.

The essentials are covered in Day One in case you only have one day. Day trips outside Hong Kong are left for later days because it takes time to make arrangements. Hong Kong has a lot of tourist spots to be covered so try to stick to this guide. But don't over-exert yourself. You'll miss a lot of the sparkle if you do.

Note that: A. Travel time and waiting in line can be considerable. **B.** If you want to have some clothes made by a tailor, consult one as soon as possible after you arrive. Three or four days are necessary and some hotel tailor shops open earlier than the usual 10am. **C.** Shopping should be fitted into spare moments and evenings as most shops stay open until about 8 or 10pm. **D.** If you want to go to Macau and China, for visa reasons tour group arrangements must be made by 2pm of the day before you go. Read also Day Three.

Day One: Hong Kong Island

This will include the **Peak, Aberdeen, Ocean Park** (if you wish) and **Hong Kong harbour.** Before you go, particularly if it is a weekend, phone the Jumbo Restaurant for a 12.15 *dim sum* lunch reservation (5-539111). Ask for a window table.

9am. The Peak. Start at the lower Peak Tram station, Garden Road, Central. This is a 10-minute walk from the Star Ferry. If you go by MTR, go to the Central stop and leave by the Furama Hotel exit. Walk towards the

mountain to the Hilton Hotel and then up Garden Road. The station is five minutes' walk away.

If you have hired a car, ask the driver to drop you off at the tram stop and meet you in the parking lot of the Peak Tower at the other end of the tram.

The view from the tram is increasingly impressive as you rise higher and higher. The tram was first completed in 1888, and is actually a cable-hauled funicular railway which operates two cars at a time, one from the top and one from the bottom. It can stop upon request at any of five stations along the way. The distance is 1.4 km., and at some places the gradient is as steep as 45 degrees. Aim for a seat at the lower end or by the windows on the same side as the entrance.

At the top end of the tram is the **Peak Tower** which offers a marvellous view of Central, Wanchai and, across the harbour, Kowloon. While you are up on the Peak you can visit the **Peak Tower Village,** or take a walk right round the Peak. The Peak Tower Village is within the Peak Tower building and is an arts and crafts village primarily for tourists. Traditional craftsmen, such as makers of sandalwood fans (always smell fans before buying), hand-carved wooden birds, hand-painted lanterns, musical instruments, tooled leather, brassware and silk paintings can be seen at work. Prices are reasonable, and the village is open from 10am to 6pm.

The complete circular route around the Peak on foot takes a leisurely hour. It is a little over three kilometres, mostly across level ground. Along Lugard Road you will see the harbour, Green Island and, more distantly, the islands of Peng Chau and Lantau.

Continuing around you will see the islands of Cheung Chau and Lamma. In the haze beyond are the islands of China. Lugard Road becomes Harlech Road on the west side. Below you can see the oldest reservoirs on the island, built in 1864. Aberdeen is easily distinguished by its floating restaurants and crowded harbour. Harlech Road leads back to your starting point. To the right is the charming old outdoor Peak Cafe, the atmosphere of which partly compensates for the appallingly slow service.

When leaving for **Aberdeen** try to go by taxi as public transport could take an hour or more. Tell the driver 'Aberdeen Centre' if he doesn't understand 'Aberdeen Pier.' If you can't get a taxi, take the tram to Central or any of the public buses down to Causeway Bay. From there take a taxi or the No. 70 bus from Central or the 72 from Causeway Bay. Once in the Aberdeen Centre area, walk over to the pier so you will know where it is and decide how much time to leave yourself for wandering around the stores. Then go back for a look around the open market.

If you have a driver, tell him to meet you at 1pm at the *other* Jumbo Restaurant pier off Shum Wan Road, near Wong Chuk Hang Estate. He should take time for some lunch.

Despite its litter and squalor, Aberdeen is an interesting fishing community where many families still live on boats. Well before 1841, it was a pirate's lair and later a harbour for servicing ships. Aberdeen has recently seen considerable development: the area around the harbour is being reclaimed for cargo handling and for a road to relieve the congestion on Aberdeen's main street. Private developers have put up skyscrapers like Aberdeen Centre which comprises residential flats and stores.

A new modern market building was opened in 1983 and is worth visiting if you like native markets. From the pier walk through Aberdeen Square on your left and then right to a white building with red trim and a few circular windows marked Aberdeen Complex. The fresh meat and vegetable market is through the doors marked 'Aberdeen Market'. Outside in the streets you may come across red candle-lit altars with smoking incense, a noodle-making factory, a herbalist's shop, an open-air barber shop and a professional letter-writer. As you walk around, listen for the clack of the wooden abacus which is still used for calculating.

Touring Aberdeen Harbour

There are several ways of touring Aberdeen harbour. One is to hire a sampan for half an hour from one of the women at the pier. The asking rate is HK$30 so try to haggle for less. Make sure you get a sampan with seats and shelter from the sun or rain. Pay at the end of the trip. Another is to take the Jumbo Restaurant ferry. You will not see as much as from a sampan but it is free.

Aberdeen harbour is about 2 km. long and you should be able to cover it in 30 minutes by sampan. Ask the sampan driver to go first to the right. The number of boats varies according to fish, festivals and foul weather. A trip here is a trip back through time, radar, TV sets, generators and engines apart. Children and dogs grow up here sometimes without setting foot on land. Laundry and salted fish hang out to dry together. Small sampans, some full of groceries, drinking water or cooked food, service the boats.

A sampan driver will not be able to give you a commentary with your guided tour, so do your reading along the way. Once out in the channel, look up on the right to the old cemeteries on the hillsides.

A. At the mouth of the harbour on **Ap Lei Chau Island** is the generating plant that provides most of Hong Kong's electricity. Ap Lei Chau ('Duck's Tongue') was developed only after the connecting bridge from Aberdeen was completed in 1980. The island is a great place for boats — one whole side is filled with boats being built, repaired or demolished. The housing estate is now home to 26,000 people. The other side of the island facing the sea is barren save for an oil storage depot.

B. Turn round at the generating plant. When you pass your starting point, you will see to the right a series of small, brightly decorated, **floating restaurants** and fishermen's meeting halls. You will then pass under the Ap Lei Chau Bridge (C). To the left is the new road blazed across reclaimed land.

D. The new **Aberdeen Marina Club** is on the left after the bend to the right. The moorings are accessible by walkways. Entrance fees for this private club are a minimum of HK$145,000.

E. Equally imposing are the three floating food palaces: the **Sea Palace,** the **Jumbo Restaurant** and the **Taipak.** The last-named is the oldest, but the most popular is the Jumbo Restaurant which was completed in 1976 and can accommodate 2,000 diners. The cheapest food is *dim sum* for breakfast, lunch or teatime, 7am to 4pm. Food here is very variable, ranging from mediocre and over-priced to superb and great value.

The interior of the Jumbo is as gaudy and gilded as the exterior and a stop here is imperative. In each hall opulent chandeliers, tiled mosaic and carved gold thrones assault the eye.

F. The **Aberdeen Boat Club,** a small three-storey white building to the right of the marina, is another private recreation club. Founded in 1967, it has a restaurant, swimming pool, boat moorings and other facilities. Next to it is a public dock and adjacent to that one of the many marine police stations. Many of the patrol boats seeking to stem the influx of contraband and illegal immigrants are based here. Sometimes they bring isolated islanders to hospital.

Flying dolphins at Ocean Park

G. Beyond the police station is a row of **boat-building factories** and several lines of pleasure boats. Moorings in Hong Kong are free for fishermen but for these privately-owned boats a mooring can cost more than HK$100,000 to buy or around HK$1,300 a month to rent.

H. If the water isn't too choppy and you have the time, you might want to venture outside the stone breakwater and see one of the longest escalators in the world; its total length is 257 metres. It was built to provide an alternative route to the important attractions on the headlands of Ocean Park.

12.15. Lunch. Your sampan can drop you at the Jumbo Restaurant for *dim sum*. Choose off the trolley or ask for *char siu bow* (steamed barbecued pork buns), *shiu mai* (pork and shrimp), *har gar* (shrimp) or *au yuk* (beef balls). Order three different dishes per person as each helping is quite small.

The next stop is at **Ocean Park,** not far from the junks. But before you leave the restaurant, telephone 5-532244 and check if all the things you want to see are open, and that the price is right. Although the views and scenery are spectacular, Ocean Park is primarily for children or for those people interested in marine life, and you may wish to miss it all completely.

After lunch, take the ferry to the pier marked Jumbo that you can see as you leave the restaurant. Once ashore, follow the road as it bears right and then turn left on Shum Wan Road. Turn left again on Nam Long Shan Road three blocks along, then a right on to Wong Chuk Hang Road. Ocean Park is a 15-minute walk or a three-minute taxi ride. If the escalator is operating, you are in luck.

1.30. Ocean Park. If the escalator isn't operating, then go to the main entrance off Wong Chuk Hang Road, and from there to the cable car. The **Ocean Theatre** performances are generally at 2pm. As it could take 30 minutes to get to the headland, where the performances are held, there is no time to lose.

Ocean Park features the best aquarium in the region: the **Atoll Reef** is a well-kept 9-metre deep tank, with 30,000 tropical fish, 300 different species including 150 kg. sharks and stingrays, and 50 kg. garoupas. Windows allow you to see it from various underwater levels.

Attractions for children include a bird show and a petting zoo. By late 1983 there should also be an **Adventure World** for the under-12 set, roller coaster-type rides and a Chinese crafts village.

Instead of Ocean Park, you may prefer a tour of **Hong Kong harbour.** You can do this on your own or take a group tour (details further on). If you finish by 5pm, end your sightseeing on the Kowloon side with an elegant afternoon tea in the lobby of the **Peninsula Hotel.** It occupies a prime site along the waterfront two blocks to the right of the Star Ferry pier. Alternatively you might go for a drink at the **Regent Hotel,** four blocks to your right and there enjoy a stunning sunset view of the harbour.

To get from Ocean Park to Central, take any public light bus marked 'Central' from the bus stop to the left as you leave the main entrance of the park. Or cross over the main road in front of the park by means of the overpass to your left. Beside it on the other side is a bus stop. Take the tunnel bus No. 70. The fare is HK$1.40.

Homework for tomorrow is to make a reservation for a table by the window for 12.15pm at **La Ronda** in the Furama Hotel, 5-255111, and look into the Macau and China travel arrangements if desired.

Hong Kong Harbour

At the very least, sail part of this lively 59.5 sq. km. harbour, the world's seventh busiest port. You will see some of the 10,000 ocean-going ships that come here each year. Freighters stay an average of 2.6 days, container ships 15.5 hours.

Group tours can be arranged at **Blake Pier** next to the Star Ferry. The **Watertours** boat leaves at 3.15. Alternatively wait a while and take the popular **Sunset Cruise** later on from here or from the **Kowloon Pier** by the Star Ferry on the other side. Phone 3-686171.

You don't have to take a group tour. The **Star Ferry** with its great view of Victoria Peak is one of the most famous rides in the world. It takes seven minutes and is cheap. If you want to do more than that, take any of the ferries from Central. The ferries to Lantau and Cheung Chau are particularly good as they pass through **Western Anchorage,** where most of the ships are'moored. Their piers are a few hundred metres to the right as you leave the Star Ferry pier on the Hong Kong side. Walk along the elevated walkway to the end. The trip will take about an hour.

A great experience, if a little extravagant, is to hire or take the dinner cruise on the 110 ft. *Wan Fu*, the Hilton Hotel's brigantine. This is a copy of the two-masted sailing ships used by the British Navy to chase pirates here. Telephone 5-233111.

A multiplicity of craft abound in the harbour, including ocean-going ships from all over the world, many with a yellow funnel on which is a yellow star under a red horizontal stripe. Along with the five-star red flag this indicates that the ship is from China. Smaller boats with Chinese characters in front of the licence number are also from China.

Marine Department launches with red tops and black bottoms are used for cleaning the garbage out of the harbour. Look for sailing junks.

Of the many places seen from the water along the Kowloon side from west to south-east, important to note are:

1. **Tsing Yi Island,** joined by a bridge to the mainland. This has oil storage tanks and oil rigs under construction. One of the dockyards for repairing ships belongs to China.

The Star Ferry terminal on Hong Kong Island

2. **Kwai Chung,** 50.5 hectares, the largest container port in Asia. It looks like a gaggle of red, metal, long-legged, long-necked dinosaurs with tiny heads.

3. The huge cream and green development of middle-class flats is **Mei Foo Sun Chuen,** behind which to the left is the pagoda of **Lai Chi Kok amusement park** and the **Sung Dynasty Village.** The Village is well worth seeing.

4. Past Mei Foo are shipyards. Note the ferry pier at **Sham Shui Po.** In this area is the prison where many Allied soldiers were held by the Japanese during the war.

5. **Stonecutter's Island** is across from Sham Shui Po and Mei Foo. It belongs to the British Army and is out-of-bounds to visitors. Its cream-coloured one- and two-storey buildings make it an anachronism in the middle of the high-rise city. Nearby is the spot where the rusting hulk of the liner *Queen Elizabeth I* lay for several years before being salvaged.

6. The ferry pier in Mongkok is at **Tai Kok Tsui** at the north end of the Yau Ma Tei typhoon shelter. From this pier boats take passengers to the overnight ferries for Guangzhou and Shanghai, which lie moored in the harbour. A ferry goes from Tai Kok Tsui to Blake Pier in Central.

7. **Yau Ma Tei Typhoon Shelter.** Some boat tours go through this shelter. Look for a forest of metal cranes behind a sea wall. Many of the craft here are lighters used for unloading bigger ships while some are working junks

Night clubs in Wanchai

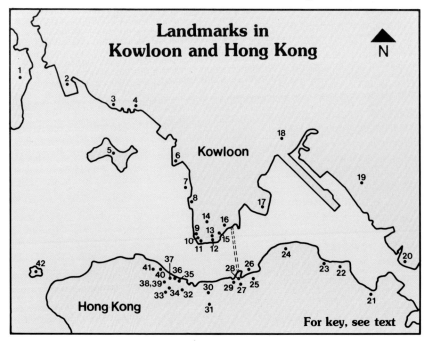

and sampans. Many families live on these boats but Aberdeen harbour is larger and more colourful.

8. The Yau Ma Tei **Vehicular Ferry** is one of several ferries that take trucks and cars across the harbour. Until the Cross-Harbour Tunnel was completed in 1972, these were the only means of getting a vehicle across the harbour.

9. **Harbour City.** This complex of hotel, residential and office blocks is expected to be almost complete by the end of 1983. The buildings curving towards the harbour are residential blocks; the one curving away is Ocean Centre. The completion of Harbour City and its connecting links with Ocean Terminal, Ocean Centre and the Hongkong Hotel make this area the largest shopping facility in Hong Kong, with a total of 600 shops and 17 restaurants. Days could easily be spent within its cool confines. Harbour City also boasts a moveable sidewalk at present more than 500 metres long but still growing. Stores are open from 10am to about 8pm daily.

10. Passenger cruise ships frequently berth at **Ocean Terminal.** Four berths, two on each side, are available at about HK$21,000 each for any part of 24 hours. Larger ships need two berths apiece.

11. The end of the **Star Ferry Pier** here was smashed by a ship during Typhoon Hope. The Hong Kong Tourist Association has an office in the building where you can pick up brochures and get answers to most of your questions. The clock tower is all that remains of the historic railway station. A police station is above the trees to its right.

12. **The Space Museum,** distinctively hemispherical, is primarily for school children. If you get tired of walking around, a look at its hour-long 360° movie on soft, comfortable chairs provides a perfect respite. Between the clock tower and the Space Museum, the Urban Council is building a 2,500-seat concert hall, a theatre and a museum of art. All should be completed in 1986.

13. Beyond the Space Museum is the **Peninsula Hotel,** an institution in Hong Kong. It was opened in 1928 in spite of labour strikes, and in the midst of a spillover of anti-foreign sentiment from China. British troops were billeted in the hotel before it was even opened. It is one of the finest hotels in Hong Kong.

14. **Nathan Road** was once known as 'Nathan's Folly'. A wide, tree-lined and at that time completely unnecessary three-mile highway, it was built in the early 1900's during the governorship of Sir Matthew Nathan. The lower part is sometimes referred to as the 'Golden Mile' because it bisects the colony's liveliest shopping, hotel and entertainment district.

15. The edifice of pink granite and dark glass is the **New World Centre.** This has two hotels, 15 floors of offices, 1,000 flats, 231 shops and 24 restaurants and bars. The building with the huge two-storey lower windows is the **Regent Hotel,** one of the best and most expensive in the city. From the Space Museum to the inverted pyramid on the right runs the **Tsim Sha Tsui**

Promenade, a lighted, public walkway over the water that's ideal for early morning jogging or after dark romantic strolling.

16. The five waterfront buildings here (three with dark mirrored walls and the Shangri-La and Holiday Inn Harbour View hotels) are part of the **Tsim Sha Tsui East** complex. This is so new that many taxi-drivers don't know it by that name. A brand new city built partially on reclaimed land, Tsim Sha Tsui East contains offices and stores, some of them still empty. The hotels here are top-class and, in addition to those mentioned above, include the Royal Garden and Regal Meridien. **Tsim Sha Tsui Centre** has the best shopping of all. The Immigration Department is located at 61 Mody Road.

Behind and to the right of the complex are the red brick walls of the **Hong Kong Polytechnic,** a post-secondary school with about 12,000 full-time students. The building with the carpark on top is **Kowloon Station.** Trains to the New Territories or to Guangzhou in China are boarded here. The inverted pyramid in front of the railway station is the new 12,000-seat **Hung Hom stadium,** the largest indoor meeting place on Kowloon side. It is used for cultural presentations, circuses, ice shows, rock concerts and sports.

17. **Hung Hom** is an industrial district important to visitors because many of the best clothing factory showrooms are here.

18. **Kai Tak** International Airport. A field here was first used by aircraft in 1928. The runway that stretches out into the harbour was first built in 1958 and extended across reclaimed land in 1975.

19. **Kwun Tong** industrial district, the end of the MTR line.

20. **Lei Yue Mun** is noted for its dumpy restaurants and delicious, pick-your-own fish meals. (See 'Adventurous Eating', page 72.) The harbour is at its narrowest at this point.

Across on the Hong Kong side, east to west:

21. **Shaukeiwan,** one of the oldest fishing villages and a former pirates' den, now at the end of the tram line.

22. **Taikoo Shing,** a private, middle class housing estate with skating rink. The Island Eastern Corridor, a four-km. long six-lane highway built on land-fill, runs from here to Causeway Bay. This section should be completed in 1984. Another section from Taikoo Shing to Shaukeiwan is expected to be finished in 1985. Both should greatly relieve the traffic congestion in this area.

23. **Quarry Bay.** Industrial area. It was here that the Japanese landed during their first invasion of Hong Kong. The hills above are part of Taitam Country Park which covers one-fifth of Hong Kong Island.

24. **North Point.** Industrial, commercial and residential area.

25. **Victoria Park,** one of Hong Kong's largest parks, with a public swimming pool, jogging trails, sports grounds and a statue of Queen Victoria.

26. **Causeway Bay Typhoon Shelter.** Swish pleasure boats and the Royal Hong Kong Yacht Club, Kellett Island. Sampans provide venues for more adventurous eating.

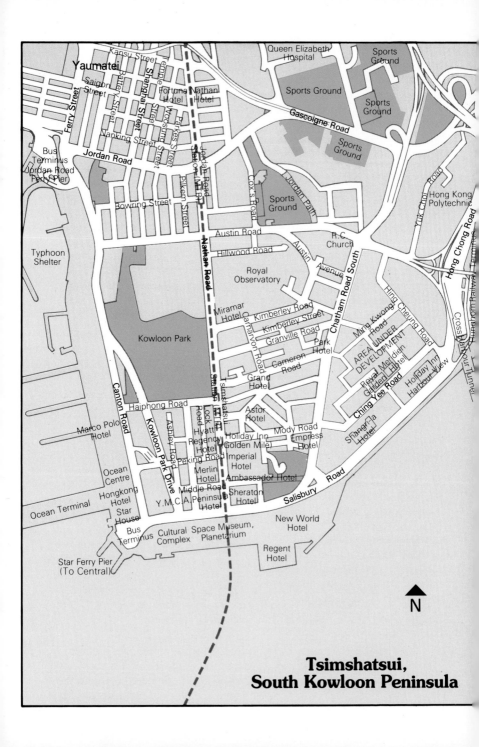

**Tsimshatsui,
South Kowloon Peninsula**

The egg-shaped dome of the Space Museum

27. Behind the **Yacht Club** are the Excelsior Hotel, the World Trade Centre and the Palace Theatre. The cinema is the best and most expensive in town.

28. The **Noon Day Gun,** located between the World Trade Centre and the Yacht Club, is still fired once a day to mark the time. This tradition originated over a century ago and has only once been broken, during the Japanese occupation. It is also fired with much ceremony at midnight on New Year's Eve.

29. The **Cross-Harbour Tunnel Entrance.**

30. **Wanchai** is known to every sailor in the world and every soldier who has ever been on R&R (Rest and Recreation) here. Naval ships are moored in this part of the harbour. It was once home to a veritable army of prostitutes and bar girls, especially during the Vietnam War. The most famous institution here is the **Luk Kwok Hotel,** associated with the movie *The World of Suzie Wong* starring William Holden and Nancy Kwan. (See Arts and Entertainment.) The Luk Kwok has become a more than respectable hotel and is recommended for those on a tight budget. The food is good, and the staff are friendly and helpful.

31. Office buildings are spreading into Wanchai. The cylindrical building on the hill is the **Hopewell Centre,** Hong Kong's tallest structure with 66 floors. On top is a revolving restaurant with a good view of the nearby **Happy Valley Race Course.** It is a good place to eat but charges appropriately up-

market prices.

32. The dark-mirrored buildings over the **Admiralty/Queensway** MTR station are typical of the architecture of the late 70's and early 80's. In 1982, gold-coloured buildings started appearing. The one here is the **Far East Finance Centre.** Its walls of reflective double glazing glass from Belgium are reputed to be made with genuine gold dust.

33. The building rising to the left of the Hilton Hotel is the **Bank of China** building. Directly behind the Star Ferry building is the new headquarters of the **Hongkong and Shanghai Banking Corporation.** The funnel-shaped structure is the headquarters of the British armed services in Hong Kong. It is designed to be sealed off in case of emergency and is more stable than it appears.

34. The **Furama Hotel** has a revolving restaurant, in the protruding lip. It has the best view of what is left of the historical buildings in this area.

35. The **City Hall** is the venue for marriage ceremonies, concerts, and art and industrial exhibitions. It also houses a public library and museum. In front of it is Queen's Pier.

36. The **Star Ferry** goes from here to Tsim Sha Tsui and Hung Hom.

37. The building with the round windows is **Connaught Centre,** probably the most useful of landmarks. The headquarters of the Hong Kong Tourist Association is on its 35th floor. In front of it is the main **Post Office** and to the right is **Blake Pier.** This is a public pier, a good place for enjoying the breeze.

38. To the right of Blake Pier is **Exchange Square,** still under construction. On completion in 1985, it will be home to the four local stock exchanges.

39. The **Central Bus Depot.**

40. Piers for ferries to **Outlying Districts.** To their right is the new Macau Ferry terminal that should be completed by the end of 1984.

41. Temporary Macau Ferry terminal. After 7pm the car park here becomes the **Poor Man's Night Club,** complete with food and hawker stalls. It is worth a browse if you're in the neighbourhood, though Temple Street night market has more goods for sale. At the terminal you can usually see jetfoils, jet catamarans, hydrofoils and ferries. A bare green patch on the hillside is all that's left after a recent disastrous landslide, the result of a typhoon.

42. **Green Island** is at the mouth of the harbour. The island has a marine police station and is now used to store explosives. Goats introduced by Gurkha troops still live on the island.

Day Two

Read this the night before in case you have to make some arrangements.

If you haven't done so already, reserve a table by the window at La Ronda Restaurant, Furama Hotel, telephone 5-255111. You can also book the afternoon tour to the Sung Dynasty Village if you wish.

Today we suggest Stanley Market, a revolving restaurant for lunch, and then the Sung Dynasty Village.

9.30-10am. Stanley Market opens. Count on 40 minutes at least to get there. This is the best time to arrive as it gets very crowded later especially on weekends. Bring bathing suit and towel if the weather is good and you want to try a beach. A hire car is ideal but a No. 6 or 260 bus from Central will take you. The stop on Connaught Road by the City Hall may be the most convenient. Before 8.20 it should be easy to get a seat up front on the top deck.

The bus takes you along the Queensway past the gold building and the Admiralty MTR station, and then along **Queen's Road East,** formerly a colonial red light district, and now a good place to buy Chinese-style furniture. On the right is an old temple, post office building and Hopewell Centre, the highest building in town.

After the turn right onto **Stubbs Road,** you pass on the left a **Sikh temple** and then the old **colonial cemetery.** Below you is Happy Valley where you can glimpse the race track. Further up the hill beyond the cemetery, you might be able to see horses exercising on a rooftop.

After the roundabout and more climbing, your bus will pass the public **Hong Kong Tennis Club** and the private **Hong Kong Cricket Club.** Once over the crest of the hill, start looking to the right. You will see the Spanish-style homes of the ultra wealthy (count the Rolls-Royces in the driveways) and, down below, **Deep Water Bay,** a favourite swimming beach, and the Royal Hong Kong Golf Club. This is where parts of the movie *A Many-Splendoured Thing* were filmed. You might also catch a distant glimpse of Aberdeen.

The bus then turns left down to **Repulse Bay,** an expatriate enclave of expensive flats and houses. It used to be an important tourist attraction, but progress has stunted that side of its character. It has one of the most popular beaches, and a stop here on the way back is always well advised. More buses are available from the other direction.

On the hill out of Repulse Bay, look back to the right to catch a glimpse of the water. The colour is sometimes incredibly green and striking. The next community, **Chung Hom Kok,** is on a peninsula to the right. Seven minutes after leaving Repulse Bay, you come to the Stanley intersection at Stanley Gap Road. Your bus turns right down the hill. Get off for the market when you see several covered bus stops. Your bus goes on to the maximum security prison.

Stanley has one of the best markets for bargain-priced sports and casual wear. For non-shoppers it also has a good beach, wind-surfing and one of the

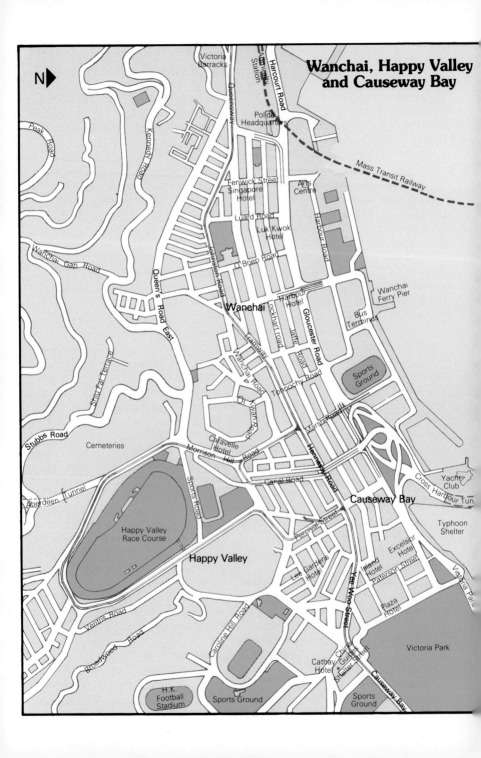

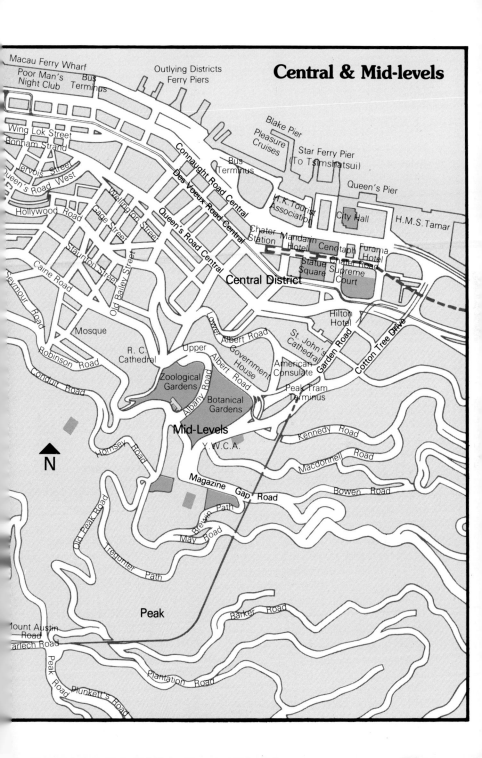

Central & Mid-levels

Macau Ferry Wharf
Poor Man's Night Club
Bus Terminus
Outlying Districts Ferry Piers

Wing Lok Street
Bonham Strand
Jervois Street
Queen's Road West
Hollywood Road
Connaught Road Central
Des Voeux Road Central
Blake Pier
Pleasure Cruises
Star Ferry Pier (To Tsimshatsui)
Bus Terminus
Queen's Pier

Wellington Street
Cage Street
Staunton Street
Old Bailey Street
Queen's Road Central

H.K. Tourist Association
City Hall
H.M.S. Tamar

Caine Road
Chater Station
Mandarin Hotel
Cenotaph
Furama Hotel
Chater Road
Statue Square
Supreme Court

Central District

Seymour Road
Mosque
R. C. Cathedral
Upper Albert Road
Lower Albert Road
Government House
Albert Road
St. John's Cathedral
American Consulate

Hilton Hotel
Garden Road
Cotton Tree Drive

Robinson Road
Conduit Road

Zoological Gardens
Albany Road
Botanical Gardens

Peak Tram Terminus

Mid-Levels

N

Hornsey Road
Y.W.C.A.

Kennedy Road
Macdonnell Road
Bowen Road

Magazine Gap Road

Old Peak Road
Tregunter Path
Brewin Path
May Road

Peak

Barker Road

Mount Austin Road
Harlech Road
Peak Road
Plunkett's Road
Plantation Road

oldest temples on the island (1767), located right next to the village incinerator! It also offers a chance of some good walking.

The shopping area is down the hill past the Park'n Shop supermarket from the bus station, then turn either left or right. There are about four blocks of shops as well as stalls on the hillside. Prices for clothes are the best in town, so haggling can be half-hearted. Chinese curios, handicrafts, brassware, oil paintings, men's shirts, ski-clothes, bed sheets, bathing suits, sneakers and Filipina, Indian, Thai and Indonesian dresses are all for sale. The Chinese-made Aran sweaters and large-sized clothes are to the right in the quonset-shaped concrete building. (See 'Shopping', page 32.)

This is a **market,** and clothes are neither ironed nor displayed with class. Some jeans are stacked several feet high so finding sizes isn't easy. Try everything on even if the dressing rooms might seen crude. Check everything carefully — the weave, seams, evenness of colour and size before buying. Have hems shortened. If you are buying for someone else, remember that several different systems are used here and 'medium' in the label means nothing.

The **swimming beach** is in the opposite direction from the market along Stanley Beach Road. Lifeguards are on duty if the weather is good. Stanley is a good place to visit during festivals as the fisherfolk here are conservative and celebrate in the traditional way.

To get to the **Tin Hau temple,** turn right at Park'n Shop, follow the curve of the street to the left after you pass the market stalls, continue to the right along the waterfront past the Seven-Eleven store, and keep going, following your nose as you bear right to the village dump. Inside, the incense masks the smells and you can see some intriguing-looking deities and probably many worshippers.

Hikers (never one person alone) should take a taxi or No. 14 bus (from the post office) for the three kilometres or so to the **Taitam Reservoir.** Get off at the gate and walk for a few metres until you see a set of stairs on your left. From here you will be climbing. If you wish, and if you have brought some bread, you could first walk to a bridge over the water in the reservoir and feed the fish. This is a most unusual experience as thousands of hungry fish break the water.

The stairs follow the paved water catchment system back to Stanley Gap Road, the intersection where you turned right to go into Stanley before. The path is longer than the road. It is a little over an hour's brisk walk on almost level ground and you can enjoy the view of **Taitam Bay** and **Turtle Cove** (identifiable by several lines of luxury townhouses). You will be walking along a part of Hong Kong's water supply system built between 1889 and 1917. Hong Kong has had a perennial water problem. It now buys fresh water from China to supplement the rain.

All will be verdant, and you might well spot some exotic wildlife — butterflies, snakes, birds and frogs. This is the natural habitat of civet cats, barking deer and porcupines, but they are rarely seen. More conspicuous are some of the last of Hong Kong's gracious old mansions — about to be torn down and replaced by the American Club — with their own tennis courts and beach. Illegal immigrants have been known to land near this road and some have hidden in the hills here.

Passing a few apartment buildings, you can take a path back to the road at Stanley Gap intersection. There at the bus stop you can see Stanley Peninsula. During the Japanese occupation, many British, American and Canadian civilians were interned either in **Stanley Prison** or **St Stephen's College.** You can see the college from here. The prison is beyond it. Walk down to your right and left along Stanley Beach Road back to the main bus stop.

If you're early there's an Anglicised pub, the Smuggler's Inn, that opens at 10am on Saturdays, and 11am on other days.

At 11.25 at the latest, take the 260 or No. 6 bus back to Central. If you go earlier, you can stop to look at the view of Repulse Bay from the hill as you leave that community. Stop at the driveway by No. 50 Repulse Bay Road, then take another bus if you have to.

Before reaching Central, get off at the stop after the Admiralty MTR stop and walk towards the harbour to the Furama Hotel.

12.15. Buffet lunch. La Ronda Restaurant, Furama Hotel. A great variety of both Chinese and European food is served. Arrive early to eat while the food is freshly cooked.

Enjoy the view. As the restaurant rotates counter-clockwise you will see an old, domed three-storey building. This is the former **Supreme Court** building which until recently was sinking because of its siting on reclaimed land. MTR construction work has drained some of the ground water from underneath, but it has now been shored up.

On the mountain behind and to the right of the Hilton Hotel is **Government House,** the official residence of the Governor. The original building was largely destroyed by the Japanese but was reconstructed after the war along much the same lines. With the harbour behind you, look down to the left of the Hilton Hotel to the low, white building. **Flagstaff House** was built in 1884 and is one of the two oldest buildings here. Up until 1978 it was the residence of the commander of the British forces. Renovations are planned and it should open in 1983 as an extension of the Museum of Art, housing an exhibit of 7th-century Chinese tea ware. One of its lawns will become a Suzhou garden.

At the time of going to press the other oldest building, **Murray House,** built in 1843, was to be taken apart piece by piece, numbered and stored for eventual restoration at another site. It is located behind the overpass to the left of the Hilton, beyond Cotton Tree Drive.

Government House nestles at the foot of Central's high-rise office blocks

The Sung Dynasty Village

It is possible to go independently and for a fraction of the price but you will lack guide, food and transport. The price does include a show, but you can only go on your own on weekdays from 6.30pm to 8.30pm and weekends from 12.30pm to 5pm. There are four tours a day on weekdays, two on weekends. Phone 3-7415111 for more information. A weekday is recommended because there are fewer other tourists around.

Count on three hours plus 30 to 45 minutes transportation each way by tour bus. If you're on your own, take the MTR to Lai Wan station. The guided tour includes a free bus ride.

The village is a full-scale model of a street in Kaifeng, China, known in the Sung dynasty as **Pien King**. It is based on a famous painting *Spring Festival on the River*. The 10th and 11th-century Sung period was one of the cultural zeniths of Chinese civilisation, noted for its arts, architecture, poetry and philosophy. This dynasty also has some tenuous historical connections with Hong Kong. The last Sung emperor was the only Chinese emperor who ever set foot here.

It would be a mistake to skip this experience because you have been or are going to China. There is nothing like this in China itself. The village was opened in 1979 and its very newness is redolent of the Sung period when commerce was at its height and buildings were being constructed. A year after it was opened, visitors could still smell the sweet fragrance of the freshly carved wood and some may still be able to enjoy this.

The 5,574-square metre exhibit is relaxing because of the classical architecture, the stream, the willow trees, the period costumes and Chinese faces. You are transported back into an 11th-century China replete with Sung dynasty food, acrobats, magicians and Chinese opera.

The entrance fee includes coupons which can be exchanged for the pastries you watch being made, or for the services of a fortune-teller. One such clairvoyant has a bird selecting a piece of paper from a pile for you, while at the temple you shake out a stick; both are traditional Chinese methods. Your fortune might sound like something out of a fortune cookie, but it's fun nonetheless. You also see a rich man's house, tastefully appointed with antiques, some of which are authentic. The vase is from the Sung dynasty.

Included in the village tour is a 70-exhibit **wax museum** with famed beauties of yore such as Yang Gui-fei from the Tang dynasty and historical personages such as the Yellow Emperor, Chiang Kai-shek and Chou En-lai. This is worth seeing if only for the stunning period costumes.

The evening is free. See Day One. And don't forget the tailor.

Day Three

Today it's Macau or China, or Macau *and* China. If it's both, then a two-day visit is in prospect. You have to decide on priorities to fit everything in or stay an extra day. Hong Kong and Macau are the only places in the world where you can arrange a one-day visit to China.

Macau

If you are going on your own, boat tickets should be booked a week in advance if they are to fit your itinerary. If you're in luck, you might be able to arrange the trip upon arrival in Hong Kong. Even if the ferry companies say they are fully booked, a well-connected hotel concierge or assistant manager might be able to help you.

Macau is 'a territory under Portuguese administration', and no longer a province or a colony. South of Hong Kong on the other side of the Pearl River, it was first settled by the Portuguese in 1557 and as a 'colony' is much older than Hong Kong. Without the benefit of space and British order, and cursed with a harbour that continually silts up, it has not developed as quickly as Hong Kong. Fortunately for tourists therefore, it still has many of its charming, pastel-coloured **Portuguese buildings** and also vestiges of old-style **Chinese architecture.**

Hong Kong's boom is echoing in the Macau streets, and what is distinctive about the enclave risks being paved with concrete. In the meantime, it still has character enough to soothe those fresh off the pavements of Hong Kong. As in Hong Kong, the population is predominantly Cantonese. More English is spoken in the streets than Portuguese. The temples are older and consequently more interesting.

Macau's Attractions

1. The duty-free **shopping** is generally cheaper than in Hong Kong but there is less variety. It is good for antiques but correspondingly good for fakes so be careful. The China products stores seem to charge about 20 per cent less than those in Hong Kong. Labour costs and rents are lower.
2. The **food** is cheaper than in Hong Kong, but not as varied. There are good Chinese, Macanese and Portuguese eating places.
3. **Gambling** is available at casinos (the Lisboa Casino is open round-the-clock). There's also jai alai nightly except weekends and public holidays on which there are matinees instead, at the Jai Alai Palace across from the ferry terminal.

Macau consists of a 5.4 sq. km. peninsula connected by a 2.06 km. bridge to the 3.6 sq. km. island of Taipa. **Taipa** in turn is connected to the 6.5 sq. km. island of **Coloane** by a 2.25 km. long causeway. Most of the total population of 400,000 live on the peninsula.

Seeing Macau

Macau can be 'done' in one day, the sightseeing in three to four hours. Those who want a more leisurely pace should spend at least two days here.

Tours are available whereby you can combine a trip to Macau with a day in neighbouring China. Or you can go on your own and book a one-day group tour from there to China. Discuss this ahead of time with your hotel tour desk, or International Tourism, Burfield Bldg., 2/F, 143 Connaught Road Central, Hong Kong (5-412011 or 5-449364). For information on Macau, phone the **Macau Tourist Information Bureau** in Hong Kong, 3-677747.

The advantage of going in a tour group to Macau is that you save yourself the trouble of getting a ferry ticket. However you may not see all you want to see. Going on your own is cheaper and more flexible, especially for four people. Budget travellers might consider taking the overnight steamer, thus saving the cost of a night's hotel room. Prices increase with the speed of the trip; the **steamer** is cheapest (2 hours) while the **hovercraft** and **jet catamaran** (75 minutes) are cheaper than the **jetfoil** (55 minutes). Trips at weekends and at night cost the most.

The **jetfoil** is the most convenient way to travel. Tickets can easily be booked at Ticketmate in the Tsim Sha Tsui MTR station between 8am and

Jetfoil speeding to the Portuguese enclave of Macau

4pm. Other tickets are not so easily acquired. For these you have to go to the Macau Ferry terminal and buy a return ticket. Since there are two and maybe three different boat companies, this can get a little complicated and time-consuming. Travellers have been known to be stranded for a day in Macau because they did not have return tickets. This may be a problem on busy weekends and holidays. The booking office is open from 9am to 5pm but the hydrofoil booking office is closed from 1 to 2pm for lunch. For ticket information telephone 5-457021 (jetfoil and steamer), 5-242841 or 5-457021 (hydrofoils).

The Macau Ferry pier is on Hong Kong Island, almost a kilometre to the right as you leave the Star Ferry. If you walk, take the elevated walkway to the end and then continue for a further 200 metres.

The timing of your one-day trip will probably be determined by the availability of transport. Aim to arrive no later than 9am in Macau. That means leaving Hong Kong before 7.45am.

Once the ticket problem is solved, the trip should be problem-free. Check in at the ferry pier 15 minutes before departure, with passport and ticket in hand. Sign your Hong Kong departure card. Make sure you fill out a Macau immigration form on the boat before you arrive or you will hold up the queue. No visas are required for most nationalities for stays of up to three days, or up to seven days for Commonwealth subjects. No health certificate is needed.

Hong Kong money is accepted at par in Macau by everyone. You can 'make' three per cent by changing Hong Kong dollars into Macau patacas at the money-changers at the Lisboa Hotel. The official rate is $103 Macau patacas to $100 HK dollars. However, change whatever Macanese money you have back into Hong Kong dollars before you leave Macau.

Taxis are usually waiting at the Macau pier. The best way to sightsee in three hours is by taxi. Pedicabs are fine except they are slower and if it rains you can't see anything. As pedicab drivers don't speak much English and will not climb hills, you are better off hiring one later.

Touts will approach you just outside the ferry pier offering an English-speaking taxi-driver. The going price is M$30 to M$40 an hour. Four people can fit into a cab. Agree on at least three hours, maybe three-and-a-half or four. A cheaper driver who speaks no English can still take you to the places listed here but won't be as helpful.

Worth including in your tour are:

1. **Bela Vista Hotel** via the Rua da Praia Grande. On the way you will pass the **Jai Alai Palace.** Jai alai (pronounced 'high a-lie') is a favourite ball game in Latin countries.

You also pass by the main grandstand for the Grand Prix, a two-day international automobile race usually held in November. On the left is the **Outer Harbour,** protected by a seawall. Further along on the right is the new **Presidente Hotel.** Adjacent is the gold and white, castle-like **Lisboa Hotel.** The circles represent Chinese money. Apart from the casino, the hotel offers a 24-hour-a-day coffee shop and restaurant and a children's playland. Both are good hotels, the Lisboa being more convenient for gamblers.

The bridge on your left goes first to Taipa Island and beyond that to Coloane. On the left also is the **Praia Grande,** a good place for an evening stroll or morning jog. After the turn to the left is a striking, low, pastel-pink building, the presiding governor's office, and once the home of its architect, a Portuguese nobleman. Nearby is the **Tourist Office.** Stop if you want some information particularly if you are thinking of bicycling on Taipa in the afternoon. The address is Travessa do Paiva.

On the horizon, ahead and to the right, is the Bela Vista Hotel, a three-storey, light green and white hotel with balconies. It was built in the late 19th century, and some visitors prefer to stay there because of the charm and the view. The rooms are huge and cheap. Stop for a few minutes and look at the lobby, then walk through the dining room to the balcony. It is typical of a world long past.

2. **Penha Hill.** This will give you some idea of the layout of the peninsula. China is to the west on the other side of the **Inner Harbour.** The bridge is to the east and Taipa Island south.

3. The **Pousada de Sao Tiago** built on the **Fortress of Barra** (1629) is a beautiful little inn. It was opened in 1982 and has 23 rooms. It is the best

and most expensive lodging place on the peninsula. You may want to come back for tea, a meal, or overnight. The entrance is a stairway through a cave. The hillside is incorporated into the design too. Look at the coffee shop and garden adorned with blue and white Portuguese tiles.

4. **The Temple of the Goddess A-Ma.** This goddess, after whom Macau is named, is related to Tin Hau, the goddess of the sea, in Hong Kong. The temple is 600 years old and feast days fall in March or April. Look into all the rooms. Funeral customs in Macau seem to be more elaborate than in Hong Kong. On the altars you might find real food, and paper models of cars, servants and houses placed in front of photographs of the recently deceased. The models will eventually be burned then used by the dead in the spirit world.

The temple also has statues of other deities including Kun Iam (Kuan Yin), the Goddess of Mercy. Look for the bas-relief stone carving of A-Ma which depicts her being brought here from Fujian province in China, after which she rose to heaven from a nearby hill.

5. The **Floating Casino.** Stop just for a peek. If you want to, go back later to gamble or eat.

6. **Avenida de Almeida Ribeíro,** the main street. Reconnoitre if you want to shop later.

7. The **Ruins of Sao Paulo** (St. Paul's) Church. The front wall is all that is left standing of what was once the most magnificent Christian structure in Asia. Built by the Jesuits with help from Japanese Christian refugees from Nagasaki in the first decade of the 17th century, the church was destroyed by fire during a typhoon in 1835. Note the remaining carvings. At the bottom of the stairs are several antique and curio shops.

8. Citadel of **Sao Paulo do Monte** (Monte Fort). This fortress was also built by the Jesuits at about the same time as St Paul's. The building which now houses the weather observatory is original. The view gained from atop the Citadel allows you to see into Zhongshan county in China, which borders on Macau. See if you can locate the other six hills of Macau from here.

9. **Camoes Museum,** though small, houses exhibits of excellent quality in the one-time headquarters of the Select Committee of the British East India Company. The museum is open daily from 11am to 5pm except on Wednesdays and public holidays. It contains Chinese paintings, pottery, sculptures and paintings by European artists.

The adjacent cemetery is for those with a more macabre sense of history. It was started in 1814 for Protestants and contains the remains of the famous colonial artist George Chinnery and Dr Robert Morrison, a missionary who translated the Bible into Chinese. An ancestor of Sir Winston Churchill is also buried here. The Portuguese had their own cemeteries.

Make an early reservation for lunch. First try **Henri's Galley** (telephone 73821), 4 Ave. da Republica, below the Bela Vista Hotel. If Henri's is full, try

Night racing at Happy Valley

Pinocchio's (telephone 07128), which opens at noon and is on Taipa Island. The **Pousada de Coloane** (08144) is third choice only because it is on Coloane, some distance away. It is very good, and the inn will send a car to fetch you, at a price. All three are noted for good Portuguese-Macanese food, such as African chicken, chilli crabs, prawns and *caldo verde* (soup).

   10. The **Garden of Lou Lim Ioc** has a moon-gate, a curved walkway (bad spirits travel only in straight lines), lotus and fish pond, and man-made 'mountains' in the best tradition of Chinese gardens. One of the mountains in the middle of the pond looks like Kuan Yin, the Goddess of Mercy.

   11. **Kum Iam Temple.** This is the local spelling of Kuan Yin, the Goddess of Mercy, one of the most popular Chinese deities. The current buildings are 400 years old. In 1844, America and China signed their first friendship and trade treaty on a circular, granite table here. Note also the two stone lions in front; each holds a ball in its mouth which gamblers rotate three times to the left for luck. Inside, among the 18 gold-lacquered figures of saints, there is supposedly a representation of Marco Polo.

   12. **Barrier Gate.** The official crossing point into China. You are not allowed close enough to take pictures but you can see trucks from China going in and out. The souvenir stalls here are full of jewellery, carvings, purses and other crafts. Some shoppers have bargained prices down to 25 per cent of the asking price, so haggling is worth it. Lots of fun. Lots of fakes too, so beware.

Ask your driver to go from here to your chosen eating place via the north-eastern seawall. You can then have a glimpse into China from the seawall and see the Chinese immigration office — a low, wide, whitish building.

Relax over lunch. The afternoon is free for more sightseeing, shopping, gambling or walks. You already know where some shops and two casinos are. Hikers can make for the **Guia Lighthouse,** an intriguing hill full of exercise equipment and a defence network of underground tunnels. Students of modern Chinese history would find the **Sun Yat-sen Memorial Home** of interest. The founder of the Chinese Republic was a doctor here before the successful 1911 revolution, and the house was built by his family to hold some of his belongings and photographs. You might also take a pedicab ride along the Praia for tea at the Pousada de Sao Tiago or the Bela Vista.

It is best to hire a car for touring the offshore islands too. Distances are vast. What few buses there are go from the bridge near the Lisboa Hotel.

Bicycles are available for rent from Taipa village. Taipa has an interesting traditional Chinese cemetery. **Fireworks factories** here have half-metre wide walls and free standing between buildings, in case of an accident. Recently, some illegal immigrants hid in one of these factories. Someone lit a match!

Taipa is the site of the **University of the East,** founded in 1981, and the harness racing **(trotting)** track.

If you are staying for dinner, try any of the above restaurants, but consider also: the **Fook Lam Moon** by the Lisboa Hotel; the **New Palace Restaurant** in the Floating Casino for seafood (phone 74480); the **Chiu Chau Restaurant** or **Four Five Six** (Shanghainese) in the Lisboa Hotel (telephone 77666).

For more information on Macau, phone the tourist office, 71638 in Macau, or 3-677747 in Hong Kong.

If you arrive back in Hong Kong after 7pm and still have time and energy, go to the left of the Macau Ferry pier to the **Poor Man's Night Club.** Hawker stalls there are filled with cheap clothes, belts, handbags and jewellery.

China

It is possible to go to China on your own without a group tour for one day but it is not practical for the average short-term tourist. You require more time for arranging the trip, and much more money.

You cannot get an individual travel reservation for anywhere in China without first getting a visa. Consult Sidney Chee at United (Taishan) Travel (3-849269), or Paulus Ng at Silkways (5-410078), or call the Travellers Hostel (3-687710). Give them at least 48 hours' notice, preferably more. It is technically possible to take an early flight to Guangzhou, spend eight hours there, and return on the late flight.

If you want to spend longer than one day in China, there are other tours available. See your hotel tour desk or the above. For the majority of tourists who are here for less than a week, we strongly recommend the one-day conducted group tour to China. Of the two possibilities, the most popular is **Zhongshan** (also known as Chungsan) or **Shiqi** (Shek Kei). The other tour to **Shen Zhen** (Shum Chun), on Hong Kong's northern border, takes you to a new town where industrial and residential projects are rapidly developing. You visit the reservoir that services Hong Kong, an arts and crafts store and a kindergarten; a total of five hours is spent in China. The Shen Zhen tour is only recommended if you can't go by boat and you're desperate to set foot in China.

Zhongshan borders on Macau. At press time, tours went first to Macau (a little over an hour's ride), and then entered China through the Barrier Gate, built in 1849. Plans are afoot for a direct Hong Kong-China ferry service.

Chinese border formalities take up to half an hour. Your guide carries one group visa and your passport is inspected but not stamped. A short customs declaration form has to be filled out, the duplicate of which must be returned to Customs on your way out. Money can be changed here but you don't really need it. You only need money for shopping and most places will accept Hong Kong dollars at the rate of HK$3 to one Chinese yuan. There isn't all that much to buy.

The immigration office is in the Gong Bei section of **Zhuhai** Special Economic Zone. SEZ's in China are restricted areas where industries are being developed in cooperation with foreign corporations who receive economic incentives not available in the rest of China. At the border of Zhuhai, about 10 minutes' ride away, you will pass a checkpoint before entering Zhongshan county. The whole tour involves a 120-km. bus ride and about seven hours in rural China.

For more information contact the tour desk in your hotel or International Tourism, telephone 5-412011 or 5-449364 in Hong Kong or 86522 in Macau, or China Travel Service, telephone 5-259121 in Hong Kong or 88922 in Macau.

Don't expect giant Buddhas or Great Walls. In the main this is a relaxing tour past green countryside, flat rice paddies, high distant hills, water buffaloes, clusters of black brick village houses and long, narrow commune buildings. In some of the villages, tall three- and four-storey towers, originally built in pre-communist times as lookout points, are reminders that bandits and tigers once roamed this area. The relatively large farm houses, especially those over one storey high, indicate that a lot of money has been, and continues to be, sent here from abroad. You may notice new village houses and television antennae which are probably the result of recent new agricultural incentive policies.

Compared to many places in China, this is a wealthy area. Only a few miles to the west is **Taishan,** the county from which the earliest Chinese immigrants to America, Canada and Australia departed.

The first stop is at **Cuiheng village,** 32 kilometres from the border. This was the birthplace of Dr Sun Yat-sen, the leader of the republican revolution which overthrew the Manchu dynasty in 1911. You are encouraged to wander around the Sun Yat-sen Memorial Middle School, and some of the most elegant-looking school buildings in China. These were built in 1934. Don't interrupt the classes.

Nearby is the site of Dr Sun's birthplace in 1866. The original house was eight metres by four metres and mud-brick. This was replaced by the house Dr Sun himself designed and in which he lived from 1892 to 1895. The exterior of the current house is Moorish rather than Chinese but the interior is typical of wealthy homes in the area — bare black brick walls, a carved and gilded family altar, an altar table, square uncomfortable chairs and wide mosquito-netted beds. In the kitchen is a huge wok set into a wood-burning stove — all that is necessary for cooking a six- or seven-course meal. In the courtyard outside is the family's water source, a well. Dr Sun's brother emigrated to Honolulu and the family's fortunes appear to have improved from that time onward.

In the complex is a large **exhibition hall** detailing Sun's life in photos, paintings, newspaper clippings and copies of letters. Only part of this is in English. Dr Sun received five years' education in Honolulu, studied medicine in Hong Kong and raised money for the revolution among the overseas Chinese. He was primarily a theoretician whose ideas now form the basis of government in Taiwan, but he is also strongly revered in China. He died of cancer in 1925 in Beijing.

Also in the complex is a **reception hall** where tourists can drink tea and shop for souvenirs. There is a bookstall by the exhibit hall. A record of Dr Sun's voice speaking Cantonese can be heard.

Some tours eat lunch in the China International Travel Service hotel in Shiqi, others at a nearby hot spring resort. Both are equally good, and provide a typical local meal.

After lunch, there is usually time enough to wander around the main street of Shiqi, to poke around the shops, and to take pictures of the Ming dynasty pagoda on the hill above the town.

Shiqi is a small town, with a population of around 100,000. The quality of the goods available is not high. Some prices are lower than in Hong Kong while some of the clothes are imports from Hong Kong and therefore more expensive than there. Look at the stop as an opportunity to glimpse a way of life, not as a place to shop. Look at what is available for the local people to buy; at the sidewalk tailors, cat skins hung up to dry, bicycle repair shops, herbal medicine stores, and the incursions of western civilisation (in the form of electronic games). Enjoy the old architecture. The ground floors on the main streets are recessed to provide shelter for pedestrians from the elements.

The last stop is at a **commune.** There you can wander through one of the wealthier commune houses. But do look into other houses too for comparison. Look at the painted flowers and pastoral scenes on the exterior and interior walls, the carvings, the family photos on the wall, the consumer products such as television sets, sewing and washing machines. If possible look at the beds, some elaborate, some just a board with a straw mat.

Look also into the **workshops.** You may see commune members making baskets. Whatever you do, don't give money to the children. Tourism only began here in 1979 and the people are still very friendly and genuine.

Other Excursions

China from the New Territories Mainland

This is for people who did not go to Macau or China. The view of China from Macau is better than from here. From a hill at **Lok Ma Chau** in the New Territories you can look down at the Shen Zhen (Shum Chun) River, barbed wire boundary fences, a few commune buildings in China, and to the right in the distance, the growing number of high-rise blocks in the Shen Zhen Special Economic Zone.

The problem with going to the New Territories by road is traffic congestion. The worst days are weekends, holidays, rainy days and horse-racing days. Construction is going on at a tremendous pace and roads may be clogged with cement trucks, dump-trucks and excursion buses. It may take you considerably more than half a day by road, much of it spent sitting in a traffic jam.

Travelling by train is only a little better. Diesel trains run to Sheung Shui where you can get a short taxi ride or No. 76 bus (plus a 20-minute walk) to Lok Ma Chau. These trains currently run once every 34 minutes to an hour. It is a 65-minute ride. The situation will improve when electric trains to Sheung Shui start after the summer of 1983, with services every 10 minutes and a journey time of 35 minutes. We should then be able to recommend the trip without reservation.

In the meantime, content yourself with seeing Chinese islands in the haze from the Peak or from Po Toi Island (see 'Adventurous Eating', page 72).

You may want to take a group tour that includes Lok Ma Chau. If you want a good tour of the New Territories, take the one offered by the Hong Kong Tourist Association. It is called **The Land Between** and it takes you to the rural parts of this area, away from the traffic. It also takes you for a glimpse of China at the north-eastern border of the colony, and includes a Chinese lunch.

Lantau Island

This island is larger than Hong Kong and, in comparison, delightfully backward. It also gives you a chance to go horseback riding, hiking, seeing a small fishing village or one of the region's largest temples. If you want, you can climb Hong Kong's second highest peak (934 metres), and from there, given clear weather, be able to see Macau across the mouth of the Pearl River. You might also be able to see bits of China.

The trip is easy. Take the 7, 8 or 8.30am ferry to Silvermine Bay from the pier marked 'Ferries to Outlying Districts'. This is a 10-minute walk to the right as you leave the Star Ferry pier, Hong Kong side. Buy the 'deluxe' class ticket and head for the upper ferry deck. The trip takes one hour and on a good day you can spend the time on the outside deck taking photos. Inside, the seating is air-conditioned and snacks are available. Read the section on the harbour tour to help identify the waterfront buildings.

On the way to **Silvermine Bay** you pass Green Island, Kau Yi Island, Sunshine Island, Peng Chau and finally Hei Ling Island.

At Shek Pik Reservoir your bus starts to climb up the mountain. Part way up, you may have to get off and change to another bus. If the weather is behaving, the views of the South China Sea and the islands are stunning. At the end of the bus line is Po Lin Monastery.

The Buddhist monastery was started by a small group of monks in 1907, the official inauguration taking place in 1927. The huge buildings that you see here were built in the late 1960's. Recently, a 7,000-volume Qing dynasty Tripitaka from the Xiyuan temple in Suzhou was given to the monastery in exchange for a generous donation for repair work on a monastery in Beijing. A special building is to be erected to house the sacred Buddhist scriptures.

On a nearby hill an **image of Buddha** 35 metres high is being constructed. Probably the tallest in Southeast Asia, it will dominate the countryside when finished in 1985.

For those intending to return within 5 hours, time is at a premium, and after 30 minutes you ought to head back on the first available bus. There is a lot more to do if you stay, however. If you are interested in a **vegetarian lunch** with imitation meat dishes and lots of good vegetables, buy a meal ticket at the office to the right of the main entrance. The monastery also has simple four-bed dormitory rooms but sexes, even within families, are segregated. The price of board includes three vegetarian meals. A nearby snack bar at the tea garden does provide meat dishes if you feel deprived without, or if the MSG flavour enhancer affects you too much.

The snack bar is about 100 metres to the left as you leave the main temple gate. Follow the signs to the **tea garden** past the paddock. If you so want, you can ride some retired racehorses here. There is also a simple and clean little hostel here where sexes aren't segregated; the rooms are very small, however. There is also a youth hostel nearby.

Beyond the tea plantation is the colony's second highest mountain, **Lantau Peak,** a tame climb by mountaineering standards as there are stone steps most of the way. Buy any soft drinks you may want at the tea garden. The climb up and back can be made in less than four hours from here and is a memorable adjunct to a Hong Kong visit.

A less strenuous hike is to follow the path up to the **stupas,** the monuments on the hill above Po Lin, and then down to your right to the paved path which leads to the fishing village of Tung Chung. The stupas contain Buddhist relics, and the path is downhill all the way (it takes about 2 hours). Unless you stop at some of the other monasteries along the way there are no drinks available. There are 500 or so monks and nuns who live in 135 monasteries on this island. The climb up Lantau Peak affords more spectacular views, but this is very pleasant too if you like hiking.

Be warned that the bus service from **Tung Chung** to Silvermine Bay (Mui Wo) is not reliably scheduled, and you may have to wait an hour or so for transport. A ferry also goes from Tung Chung back to Central some time in the early afternoon or after 7pm on weekdays, and after 5pm on Sundays and holidays. There is also a ferry to the New Territories but you then have the problem of getting back to your hotel.

Since the bus stops also at the Tung Chung ferry pier, you could wait there and take whatever arrives first. Tung Chung has a few little restaurants; the one by the bridge over the river is particularly good. The remains of a Qing dynasty **fort** lie about a mile from the ferry on the bus route, but they hardly merit a special trip.

There are several good restaurants both in and en route to Silvermine Bay. **Tong Fuk Store** (5-9848329) in Pui O Village is a favourite of foreigners. Pui O is eight minutes by bus after you pass the long beach at **Cheung Sha.** This rather inelegant but very popular restaurant closes at 5pm every Tuesday and all day on Wednesdays. Otherwise it is open daily from 12 noon to 3pm and from 6 to 9pm. Bus services are more frequent from Pui O back to the ferry. Taxis are now available, but in short supply.

Tram Ride

A favourite and also cheap excursion is to take the tram to North Point. Take several dollars in small change. Try to board by the Macau Ferry pier because it's near the terminus and you really need to secure a front seat upstairs to get the most out of the ride. You may even get a cool, antique wicker seat.

The only times to avoid are during rush hours. The tram will take you parallel to the harbour from west to east at a pace slow enough for you to absorb the sights. You are roughly following the route of the new MTR line and will see here and there construction related to it. If you see something you want to spend more time studying, make a note and on the way back you can return to it.

The ride to **North Point** takes about an hour, depending on traffic. At night when buildings are lit from within, your high vantage point allows you also to see inside residential flats and stores.

Around the Macau Ferry pier you will see offices with a name lifted out of the past. A 'compradore' is a middle man, a native agent for a foreign business. The word is of Portuguese origin and grew out of the early China trade.

The tram twists around to Des Voeux Road where on the left are the two big department stores, Wing On and Sincere. On the right is the back side of the Central Market, another gory, blood-bespattered but fascinating place. You are now in **Central,** the city's financial and commercial centre. Note all the banks and jewellery stores and, to the right, the alleys full of stalls (cloth, clothes, bags, padded jackets and sweaters). The centre of town is around the ritzy Landmark on the right, built on top of Central MTR station. At lunchtime on sunny days, one can barely move in this area because of the crowds.

The Star Ferry is to the left after the swing to the right, beyond the **Mandarin Hotel.** The Mandarin's new coffee shop is a joy, a very restful place with western classical music. To the right the new headquarters of the Hongkong & Shanghai Banking Corporation, the **Hongkong Bank** for short, are under construction. The Bank of China lies across the street from the former Supreme Court building, one of the few old buildings that has thus far escaped redevelopment.

Ahead are the gold walls of the **Far East Finance Centre.** The Hilton Hotel is on the right, along with a coffee shop called Cat Street.

To the left of the Hilton lies the site for the new Bank of China building. The **Murray Building** on the right past the overpass is due to be torn down, stored and some years hence rebuilt, probably further up the hill. It is one of the island's oldest buildings. On the hill are some other older buildings, former barracks, while by the road is the new Supreme Court building.

On the left by the gold building are stores and office blocks sited over Admiralty MTR station and bus depot. The low buildings adjacent are police barracks.

You are now in **Wanchai,** an area with a growing number of offices and a diminishing number of bars. Because of its proximity to the naval anchorage, this was once a notorious rest and recreation district. It still has a lot of nightlife but it is now a shadow of its former self. The triangular building un ahead (topped by an old pagoda and a cross) is a Chinese Methodist church. You are now on **Hennessy Road.**

The stores in this area service the local residents. Look for herbal medicine stores, bird shops and tea shops. Silver-trimmed red bridal gowns and gold jewellery dress the windows. Open markets, auto parts stores and sidewalk hawkers crowd together.

Once under the Canal Road overpass by the fire station, you are more or less in **Causeway Bay,** a good place for buying sportswear. Three sumptuous but not exclusive Japanese department stores are situated here, as is **Food Street.** This consists of several blocks between the Plaza and Excelsior hotels lined only with restaurants, some of them excellent. **Victoria Park,** on the left, is one of the largest parks in town, popular for festivals and Hong Kong's infrequent political demonstrations. On the hill to the right you can see middle-class housing and squatter huts almost side by side.

Beyond the curve and the overpass at the Seven Seas Shopping Centre is North Point, an industrial, residential and commercial area, very Chinese, and rarely visited by tourists. The restaurants here are huge, occupying several floors each, and all bedecked in red and gold. The tram turns to the left off the main street, and then to the right, cutting through an open market. The end of this line is at **King's Road** and a large China Products store. You pay at the front door as you leave the tram. Browse around North Point if you wish. The most pleasant way to get back to Central is to walk from the tram terminal to the harbour (two blocks away and then to the right) where you can take a ferry to Hung Hom. And then from an adjacent pier take a ferry to Central.

View from North Point towards Causeway Bay and Central

A Bus Tour Around the Island

If you're now hooked on public transport, you can take another tram or a bus from King's Road marked **'Shaukeiwan'** and continue going in the same direction as you arrived for an around-the-island excursion. Get back to the top storey. This whole trip will take two or three hours as it involves several bus changes and waiting time. Before embarking on it, take lots of change.

About one kilometre past Cityplaza and **Taikoo Shing** (the large residential development on the left) start looking for a '14' on the bus stops. When you find it, get off and switch to a No.14 bus which passes this area every 20 or 30 minutes before 7.30pm. Don't attempt to go beyond Shaukeiwan after dark as you won't be able to see anything.

The No. 14 bus will take you through the unbelievably green and almost undeveloped eastern side of the island, past the **Taitam Reservoir** to Stanley. From Stanley, you can take a No. 73 bus to Wah Fu which takes you past Repulse Bay and the lovely Deep Water Bay area. Get off in **Wah Fu** and switch to a No. 4 bus. The No. 4 will take you along **Pokfulam Road,** past the University of Hong Kong and Queen Mary Hospital (where, as readers of A Many-Splendoured Thing will know, Dr Han Suyin used to meet her lover up above the mortuary). The same bus runs to Central.

Tiger Balm Gardens

This is open from 9am to 4pm daily and takes a minimum of 10 minutes to see. Visitors either love or hate it. It is one of the oldest tourist attractions here, a 3.2-hectare private garden built by two brothers who made their money on Tiger Balm, a menthol-based ointment that many Chinese regard as a cure-all.

The lovely mansion, the interior of which is closed to the public, is typically Chinese. Visitors can walk around the white marble or alabaster Buddha and the seven-storey **white pagoda,** the only one of its kind in Hong Kong. Less easily appreciated are the rather hideous plaster sculptures which are images of the owners' idea of hell, and of Chinese mythological animals. Some consider they spoil the garden, but children will love the caves nonetheless. The pagoda cannot be climbed but it is an ideal backdrop for travel snaps.

Yau Ma Tei, Kowloon Walking Tour

Start with the **Jade market** which is open only from 10am until about noon. This market is not just for shoppers but also for people interested in seeing a genuine Chinese institution. To get there, take the MTR to Jordan Road, leave via the Yue Hwa exit, walk three-and-a-half blocks to the right to Canton Road, then turn right.

The market sprawls along three city blocks, merchants spreading piles of 'jade' pendants, bangles and earrings along the sidewalk or on tables. Dealers crowd along the road looking at bracelets wrapped in red and white packages, sometimes haggling in the traditional manner with clandestine hand signals. The number of fingers put into the seller's hand indicates the number of dollars or hundreds of dollars the buyer is offering.

The Chinese definition of 'jade' covers any precious stone. When therefore a merchant says a piece of serpentine is 'jade' he's not necessarily lying, but he is fooling you. The western definition of jade is **jadeite** or **nephrite**. The very valuable emerald green imperial jade is jadeite. Jade can be any of several colours, is extremely hard and can't be scratched with a knife. Like most gems, it is cool to the touch.

Generally speaking, the quality of jade here at the open market is low. Some of the pieces are so cheap (HK$10) and attractive that even if they aren't jadeite or nephrite they are still good souvenirs.

Walk between the stalls and the shops and then back along the road so you can watch the dealers as they hold up pieces against the light, checking for translucency, clarity and good colour. Some dealers sell roughs which are unpolished pieces of jade. Some of these are chopped up, some with only a thin slice cut out of them, the inside of otherwise unknown quality.

If you're buying, consider the quality of the carving, and in the case of the much-valued multi-coloured jade, the artistry with which the different colours have been worked into a beautiful design. It is customary to bargain in the market. Even in one of the stores we have seen prices sliced by half the marked price. The buyer was a regular customer and it took 30 minutes of good-natured haggling. If you are a tourist, you should aim for 25 per cent reduction and be content with what you think it's worth to you.

Don't buy any expensive pieces here unless you know jade, and even then it's best to buy from a member of the Hong Kong Tourist Association. Sometimes jade is dyed to look like imperial jade. The brilliant green colour, alas, fades in about a year. Jade does turn colour with wear, and for the better. Jade is believed to protect the wearer from sickness.

Chinese Street

The area north and east of the jade market is full of traditional Chinese shops and markets. If you wish, continue walking between Canton Road and Temple Street, up to **Saigon Road.** On the way you will come across stores selling paper houses and other amenities for the dead, kites (on Ning Po Street), herbalist shops selling aphrodisiacs, wine shops with snakes in bottles, and incense shops (on Reclamation Street). Look also for shops selling altars and eight-sided Taoist mirrors (the latter are used to deflect away the bad spirits).

Aim eventually for **Public Square Street,** about six blocks parallel to and north of Jordan Road. There, turn right until you arrive at four green tile-roofed temples just before Nathan Road. These temples are dedicated to Tin Hau, Shing Wong, who is the City God, the Earth God and the protector of the local community. That the temples used to be near the waterfront is clear measure of Hong Kong's growth. The Tin Hau temple to the sea goddess is more than 100 years old. There is probably a god here for every conceivable circumstance, joyous or otherwise.

In the evening, **Temple Street** (two-and-a-half blocks past McDonald's from the Jordan Road MTR stop, and on the right) becomes a five-block night market, full of colour, especially around the temples.

Bird Market

The bird market is most easily reached from the corner of Nathan Road and Argyle Street. There is an MTR exit here. Walk two blocks west along Argyle Street to Hong Lok Street. This is an alley on the south side, not easily found.

You may have heard that Fred, the sulphur-crested cockatoo of the American TV series *Baretta*, came from Hong Kong. You may have heard also that cockatoos are cheaper here than in your own country. You may even have had the foresight to get an import licence so you can take a bird back home with you. From time to time this market does have cockatoos and parrots. It is also an interesting place to visit if you like birds, but be aware that this is an alley, not a fancy bird store, and the merchants are merchants, not veterinarians. If you are buying an expensive bird, be aware also that some birds have died within days of purchase. If you are considering making a purchase, telephone the nearby **Kowloon Veterinary Hospital** (3-851956) and explain the situation. If the merchant does not understand English, have someone at the hospital explain in Chinese that you want to take the bird to the hospital to be examined before you make a decision to buy it. If need be the store could send a clerk with you to the hospital. The hospital's address is 9 Tung Fong Street.

Chinese people love birds. You will see them taking them out for airings, and then to meet other birds in bird restaurants. The bird market here has crickets for sale as pets, another custom peculiar to the Chinese. The live grasshoppers and worms are for feeding the birds.

Temples

The temples of Hong Kong are not as old as those in Macau but some of them are well worth seeing. The most elaborate are the new sections of the Po Lin Monastery (see 'Lantau', page 111) and the new **Wong Tai Sin**

Temple. A visit to the **Man Mo Temple** in Hollywood Road can be combined with a walking trip (see below) of the antique stores.

The easiest temple to visit is the Wong Tai Sin. Take the MTR to Wong Tai Sin, and leave by the exit marked Wong Tai Sin Temple. Be prepared for the aggressive ladies selling incense and joss-sticks at the top of the stairs. If you wish, carry some loose change ready to give to beggars. Be prepared also for the 100 or so fortune-telling stalls and more incense and joss-stick sellers between the gate and the temple. We haven't found a fortune-teller here yet who speaks English, so if you want your fortune told, you'll have to bring your own interpreter. Some fortune-tellers read head and face shapes, some palm lines, and others predict according to the fortune stick you shake out inside the temple.

Wong Tai Sin Temple was opened in 1973. Despite, or perhaps because of, its youth, it is dauntingly and classically Chinese. The ambience is that of a place of humble obeisance; the shaking of fortune sticks, offering of food, burning of incense, occasional banging of gongs, worshippers kowtowing to the ground, all see to that. Visitors are usually kept out of the buildings probably because of the smoke.

The temple is a good place in which to take photographs. It has a Chinese garden, opened in 1982 with all the appropriate elements, pock-marked 'mountains', water, buildings and foliage. A small entrance fee is charged. A pretty but far from perfect copy of Beijing's nine dragons screen, waterfalls, fountains, goldfish pond and a grotto all enhance the peaceful charm. The temple buildings are set with gilded altars, lanterns and some statues. Although this is a Taoist temple, a small octagonal shrine with an eight-pointed star on the floor is dedicated to **Sakyamuni,** the Lord Buddha.

Chinese Gods

Wong Tai Sin is a god who heals illnesses and grants wishes. He is a favourite of gamblers. At New Year this temple is especially packed with worshippers seeking to influence their fortunes for the coming year. The water at the temple is believed by some to heal, and a trained herbalist is often available to dispense free advice. You may see some herbs drying in the sun.

Wong Tai Sin Temple is only one of 600 temples in Hong Kong. Most are Buddhist, some Taoist, some a mixture of both faiths. There are those experts who classify worship of **Tin Hau** and **Tam Kung,** the sea deities, as Buddhist; others who define such worship as Taoist. All we can say is that they are Chinese.

In almost every temple you will find a fair mix of deities, many of whom were originally real people. In addition to those mentioned, some of the important ones are: the **monkey god,** a mischievous rascal who was expelled by the Taoists and taken in by the Buddhists. He is a favourite of children.

The temple at Wong Tai Sin

Kuan Yin, the Buddhist Goddess of Mercy, is a bodhisattva, a being who has attained Buddhahood but has chosen to return to earth to help people. Kuan Yin has several spellings here, among them Kwan Yin and Kwun Yum. Kuan Yin was originally a male Indian god, but gradually developed into a female as she was adopted by the Chinese. She frequently carries a vase or a child. In male form, he may have 1,000 arms and eyes.

Pao Kung is the God of Justice who is also invoked to exorcise ghosts. The god **Man** as in 'Man Mo' temple is the God of Literature, and of particular import to civil servants. He is depicted holding a writing brush. The god **Mo** as in 'Man Mo' temple is the God of War, known elsewhere in China as Guan Yu, or Guan Di. He is supposed to prevent war, and is also the patron saint of policemen. Little **Shing Kung** is one of the judges of hell.

Many of the temples in Hong Kong are run by private charities. All are equipped with fortune sticks, cylindrical boxes with bamboo sticks. Watch other worshippers: as they shake the boxes, one stick will invariably come out by itself. Each stick has a number. This is taken to the caretaker who, for a fee, will exchange it for a corresponding piece of paper bearing Chinese script. In the Man Mo Temple a book of translations of these slips is considerately for sale.

For those wanting to learn more about Chinese temples, one of the intriguing ones is the **10,000 Buddhas Temple** in Shatin. Some of these deities look like cheap amusement-park statuary but at least the gilded remains of its founder are on prominent display. This temple, however, represents an excursion of three hours or so. You take the MTR first to Kowloon Tong and then the electric train to Shatin. From the station, go to your left following signs marked 'Taxi' and then start asking for directions. The path is to the right of the old black brick farm houses and then up 488 stone steps.

Antiques, Chinese Crafts and Man Mo Temple

Even if you are not interested in buying, take a walk along **Lower** and **Upper Lascar Rows** and Hollywood Road on Hong Kong Island. Explore the shops. Consider them museums or art galleries. Tell the clerks you're 'just looking'.

Look out for bridal baskets, used for the agreed-upon exchange of gifts between the families of brides and grooms, and *tankas*, the religious Tibetan teaching posters once carried by itinerant monks. Also of interest are gilded pieces of carved wood used to decorate altars, and all kinds of carved, painted and lacquered chests. The stores will also have Buddhas, porcelains, brass and cloisonné. For good Chinese paintings, drop in at Hanart at 40 Hollywood Road.

If you're more interested in rare and valuable antiques, start from Ian McLean's at 69 Wyndham Street and continue to the right after leaving that store. **Wyndham Street** leads onto the six-block long Hollywood Road. Chinese craft lovers can count on several hours of enjoyment.

Otherwise start at Lower Lascar Road about five blocks uphill above the Macau Ferry terminal, and look in on the new **Cat Street Centre.** The lower five floors are devoted to antique and curio shops as well as a permanent display of Chinese arts and crafts.

Further uphill on Hollywood Road is the Man Mo Temple, itself an antique, believed to have been built in the 1840's. The pewter, brassware and altars were made in China more than a century ago. This Taoist temple is dedicated to the gods of Literature and War. Mounted on poles on the left are the symbols of the Eight Taoist Immortals. The deer symbolizes long life. The old sedan chairs were once used to carry the main statues through the streets. They and the bell are well over a century old.

After exploring this temple and the one to all gods next door, head off to your right along Hollywood Road and enjoy browsing.

Meeting the Natives/the Locals

It is always better when you are in a new country to meet some of the local residents. They can give you valuable insights and help, and you might find some of them memorable.

In Hong Kong, friendly visitors frequently run up against British reserve and Chinese formality. You simply need to be introduced before they will chat with you. In addition, people here are busy, intensely so. If you do want to meet local people, go to a church or synagogue. Some Chinese attend English-speaking services too. If you find someone particularly interesting, invite him out for tea. Play the helpless tourist. Tell him you want to try a *dim sum* restaurant and don't know how to go about it. Could he show you and join you? Just don't be discouraged. Every year visitors pass through Hong Kong by the million; local people couldn't possibly be hospitable to all of them.

Another way to meet people is through sports. Once you get to the courts, it is relatively easy to find a tennis partner. Or you could volunteer to crew on a yacht if you know how. Look up the **Hash House Harriers** if you like to jog and drink, or locate the **Archaeological Society** or any other group that interests you. Several organisations such as the **Round Tables** organise walks for charity. Ask if you can join them. For telephone numbers, call the Community Advice Bureau.

For both men and women who don't like going to bars alone, you can meet some local residents, both Chinese and expatriate, at a unique social club called the **Up Club.** Meeting at a different watering-hole every Friday from 7 to 10pm are about 15 to 50 members, business people, professionals, government servants. A club hostess is there to introduce. Telephone 5-431037, Up Club International, 1807 Korea Centre, 119 Connaught Road Central, Hong Kong.

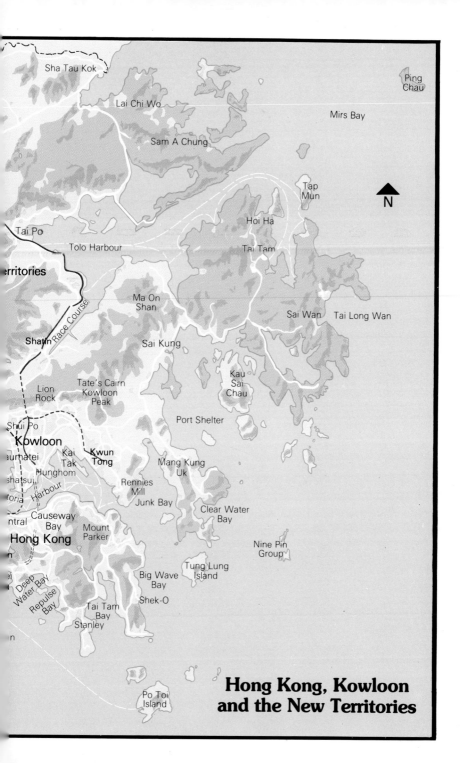

Sha Tau Kok

Ping
Chau

Lai Chi Wo

Mirs Bay

Sam A Chung

Tap
Mun

Tai Po

Hoi Ha

Tolo Harbour

Tai Tam

rritories

Ma On
Shan

Race Course

Sai Wan   Tai Long Wan

Shatin

Sai Kung

Kau
Sai
Chau

Lion
Rock

Tate's Cairn
Kowloon
Peak

Shui Po

Port Shelter

Kowloon

aumatei   Kai   Kwun
           Tak   Tong

Mang Kung
Uk

shatsui   Hunghom

Rennies
Mill

toria   Harbour

Junk Bay

ntral   Causeway
           Bay

Clear Water
Bay

Mount
Parker

Hong Kong

Nine Pin
Group

Deep
Water Bay

Tung Lung
Island

Big Wave
Bay

Repulse
Bay

Shek-O

Tai Tam
Bay
Stanley

Po Toi
Island

**Hong Kong, Kowloon
and the New Territories**

Recommended Reading

Hong Kong has spawned a large number of guide and special interest books. Most helpful for tourists are the guides published by the Hong Kong Tourist Association, many of them available free of charge. Especially helpful in preparing this book have been the following government publications: *Hong Kong Streets and Places* (for maps); *Hong Kong 1982* (the official government year book); *Hong Kong 1981 Census* (Basic Tables); and *This is Hong Kong: Temples*.

Browse through the bookstores. They all have large sections of books on Hong Kong and China. We have found valuable: Tobin's *Guide to Hong Kong Nightlife* (Gulliver Books); G.B. Endacott's *A History of Hong Kong* (Oxford); William Meacham's *Archaeology in Hong Kong* (Heinemann Asia); and Lesley Nelson's *Top Restaurants in Hong Kong* (Far East Trade Press). Han Suyin's *A Many-Splendoured Thing* (Triad Panther) is also widely available.

A convenient bookstore is the SCMP Family Bookshop at the Star Ferry, Hong Kong side. There are also several bookstores in the Ocean Terminal and Ocean Centre.

Appendix

Airlines
Air France
2104 Alexandra House (HK) 5-248145
Air India
Rm. 1002 Gloucester Tower (HK) 5-214321
Air Lanka
502 New World Centre (K) 3-696393
Air Nauru
G/F Kai Tak Commercial Bldg (HK) 5-450642
Air New Zealand
1614 Prince's Bldg (HK) 5-640123
Air Niugini
G/F, Swire House (HK) 5-242151
Alitalia
Hilton Hotel Arcade (HK) 5-237047
All Nippon Airways
2001 Fairmont House, 8 Cotton Tree Dr (HK) 5-251306
British Airways
G/F, Alexandra House (HK) 5-775023
British Caledonian Airways
G/F, Hilton Hotel (HK) 5-212353
Canadian Pacific
G/F, Swire House (HK) 5-227001
Cathay Pacific Airways
G/F, Swire House (HK) 5-640123
China Airlines
G/F, St. George's Bldg (HK) 5-243011
China National Aviation Corp.
G/F, Gloucester Tower (HK) 5-216416
Garuda Indonesian Airways
7-C Fu House (HK) 5-225033; R 5-235181
Japan Air Lines
G/F, Gloucester Tower (HK) 5-230081
KLM Royal Dutch Airlines
Fu House (HK) 5-220081; R 5-251255
Korean Airlines
G/F, St.George's Bldg. (HK) 5-235177; R 3-686221
Lufthansa German Airlines
G/F, Hilton Hotel (HK) 5-225101; R 5-212311
Malaysian Airline System
107 Swire House (HK) 5-252321; R 5-218181

Northwest Orient Airlines
St. George's Bldg (HK) 5-249261; R 5-243061
Pan American World Airways
Alexandra House (HK) 5-243081; R 5-231111
Philippine Airlines
Rm. 114 Swire House (HK) 5-227010; R 3-694521
Qantas Airways
G/F, Swire House (H) 5-242101
Royal Brunei Airlines
Rm.735 Central Bldg (HK) 5-223799
Royal Nepal Airlines
Rm. 1133 Star House (K) 3-69915
South African Airways
G/F, Alexandra House (HK) 5-775023
Singapore Airlines
1/F, Landmark (HK) 5-296891; R 5-296831
Swissair
8/F, Admiralty Centre, Tower 2 (HK) 5-293670
Thai International
2/F, World Wide House (HK) 5-257051; R 5-295601
United Airlines
3/F, St George's Bldg (HK) 5-261212

Consulates

Australia
10/F, Connaught Centre, Central 5-227171
Austria
2201 Wang Kee Bldg, Central 5-239716
Bangladesh
605 Kam Chung Bldg, 54 Jaffe Rd Wanchai 5-280325
Belgium
1803 World Trade Centre, Causeway Bay 5-7907321
Bolivia
1408 Guardian House, 32 Oi Kwan Rd 5-728393
Brazil
1107 Shell House, Central 5-257002
Burma
2424 Sun Hung Kai Centre, 30 Harbour Rd Wanchai 5-8913329
Canada
14/F, Asian House 5-282222
Chile
11/F, Hua Hsia Bldg, 64 Gloucester Rd 5-732139

Colombia
607 Nanyang Commercial Bank Bldg, 151 Des Voeux Rd, Central 5-458547
Costa Rica
C-10 Hung On Bldg, 3 Tin Hau Temple Rd 5-715846
Cuba
10/F, B Rose Court, 115 Wongnaichung Rd, Happy Valley 5-760226
Cyprus
19/F, United Centre 5-292161
Denmark
1015 Swire House 5-256369
Dominican Republic
20/F, OTB Bldg 5-727234
Ecuador
Flat C-4, 11/F Hankow Centre, 1-C Middle Rd, Kowloon 3-692235
Egypt
G/F, 20 Macdonnell Rd 5-244174
El Salvador
1517 Central Bldg 5-228995
Finland
1409 Hutchison House 5-224892
France
26/F, Admiralty Centre, Tower Two 5-294351
Germany
21/F, United Centre 5-298855
Greece
1702A Alexandra House 5-200860
Guatemala
1702 Swire House 5-248161
India
16/F, Block D, United Centre 5-284028
Indonesia
2/F, Indonesian Centre, 127 Leighton Rd 5-7904421
Iran
1901-2 Alliance Bldg, 130-136 Connaught Rd 5-414745
Irish Republic
8/F, Prince's Bldg 5-226022
Israel
1122 Prince's Bldg 5-220177
Italy
801 Hutchison House 5-220033
Japan
24/F, Bank of America Tower 5-221184

Jordan
911 World Shipping Centre, 7 Canton Rd, Kowloon 3-696399
Korea
1/F, Korea Centre 5-430224
Lebanon
14/F, New World Centre, Kowloon 3-669595
Liberia
703 Admiralty Centre, Tower One 5-295088
Luxembourg
c/o Mr Michael Bamberg 5-233111, Ext. 1200
Malaysia
24/F, Malaysia Bldg, 50 Gloucester Rd 5-270921
Mauritius
7/F, Chung Nam Bldg, 1 Lockhart Rd, Wanchai 5-281546
Mexico
2704 International Bldg, 5-454245
Monaco
c/o French Consulate, 26/F, Admiralty Centre 5-294351
Nauru
1705-1708 Kai Tak Commercial Bldg, 317 Des Voeux Rd 5-447129
Netherlands
1505 Central Bldg 5-227710
New Zealand
3414 Connaught Centre 5-255047
Norway
1401 AIA Bldg 5-749253
Pakistan
307-8 Asian House 5-274622
Panama
1212 Wing On Centre 5-452166
Paraguay
903 Hang Lung Bank Bldg 5-7905456
Peru
10/F, F Golden Plaza, 745-747 Nathan Rd, Kowloon 3-803698
Philippines
8/F, Hang Lung Bank Bldg, 8 Hysan Ave, Causeway Bay 5-7908823
Portugal
1405 Central Bldg 5-225789
Singapore
19/F, Wang Kee Bldg 5-247091
South Africa
27/F, Sunning Plaza, 10 Hysan Ave, Causeway Bay 5-773279

Spain
1401 Melbourne Plaza 5-253041
Sri Lanka
12/F, Aubin House, 171 Gloucester Rd, Wanchai 5-729271
Sweden
711 Wing On Plaza, Kowloon 3-7220333
Switzerland
3703 Gloucester Tower 5-227147
Thailand
2/F, Hyde Centre, 221-226 Gloucester Rd 5-742201
United States of America
26 Garden Rd 5-239011
Uruguay
103 View Point, Block B, 7 Bowen Rd 5-248792
Venezuela
804 Star House, Salisbury Rd, Kowloon 3-678099

Visas to the following countries may be obtained at these offices:
China
China Travel Service, 77 Queen's Rd Central 5-259121
Nepal
HQ Brigade of Gurkhas, Royal Nepalese Liaison Office 5-28933255
Taiwan
Chung Wah Travel, 1009 Tak Shing House, 20 Des Voeux Rd, Central 5-258315
United Kingdom
Immigration Dept, Mirror Tower, 61 Mody Rd, Kowloon 3-7333111

Hotels

Hong Kong has some of the best hotels in Asia, and perhaps the world, in terms of comfortable, well-equipped guest rooms, efficient and friendly service, imaginative decor, marvellous views and top notch facilities for wining, dining, meeting and relaxing.

Whichever hotel you choose in the top categories, it is likely to be a modern high-rise building with air-conditioned rooms which include private bathroom, telephone, colour television and often a refrigerator and minibar. The odds are that the views will be spectacular. Keen competition keeps the standard of service very high and most hotels have round-the-clock room service.

Hotels in the moderately priced category are clean, comfortable and efficiently staffed. They tend to be a little farther from the tourist hubs but are well served by taxis and public transport.

All hotels have good restaurants. The smaller ones might have one dining room, serving European and Chinese food. The large hotels contain some of the best restaurants in town, and much local entertaining takes place here.

The hotels are also used extensively for business meetings, conferences, art exhibitions, trade promotions and special events such as antique auctions.

Hotel List

Central District

Furama Inter-Continental 1 Connaught Rd. tel. 5-255111
An elegant high-rise with 571 rooms beside the harbour, close to ferry and MTR. It has busy meeting areas and a spectacular revolving restaurant. Rates $590-720 double.
(4 restaurants, 2 bars, revolving restaurant, disco)

Hilton 2A Queen's Rd. tel. 5-233111
Centrally located with 821 rooms, popular restaurants and superb pool terrace. It has regular dinner-theatre presentations. Rates $590-690 double.
(4 restaurants, 6 bars, pool, brigantine cruises, business centre)

Mandarin 5 Connaught Rd. tel. 5-220111
In easy reach of Central offices, a hub of local and visiting businessmen. Famed for service, restaurants and Roman-bath. It has 565 rooms at $645-945 double.
(5 restaurants, 3 bars, health club & pool, business centre)

Causeway Bay

Caravelle 84-86 Morrison Hill Rd. Happy Valley tel. 5-754455
Opposite the race course, a convenient, comfortable and moderately priced hotel, 94 rooms at $260-280 double.
(Bar, restaurant, coffee shop)

Excelsior 281 Gloucester Rd. tel. 5-767365
Next to the Cross-Harbour Tunnel and close to shops, restaurants and nightlife. Famous for its nightclub and sports facilities. Its 958 rooms are $520-710 double.
(3 restaurants, 3 bars, nightclub, tennis courts, health club)

Harbour On the waterfront, close to nightclubs, restaurants, a friendly and reasonably priced hotel with 198 rooms at $230-250 double.
(Nightclub, bar, 2 restaurants)

Hong Kong Cathay 17 Tung Lo Wan Rd. tel. 5-778211
In Causeway Bay, a quiet, comfortable hotel with 142 rooms, moderately priced at $200-230 $240-280 double.
(Restaurant, coffee shop)

Lee Gardens Hysan Avenue tel. 5-767211
Close to the nightlife and shops of Causeway Bay, the hotel has large public areas and 900 rooms at $510-620 double.
(3 restaurants, 3 bars)

Luk Kwok 67 Gloucester Rd. Wanchai tel. 5-270721
On the Wanchai waterfront and reputed to be the haunt of 'Suzie Wong', this is a comfortable and respectable 102-room hotel. Rates are $210-260 double.
(Nightclub, 4 restaurants)

Plaza 310 Gloucester Rd. tel. 5-7901021
Opposite Victoria Park and close to busy Causeway Bay, this 850-room hotel is noted for its Japanese restaurant. Rates are $500-620 double.
(4 restaurants, disco, sauna, massage)

Singapore 41 Hennessy Rd. tel. 5-272721
A hotel with 165 rooms in the heart of Wanchai with good food and atmosphere. Rates are $245-275 double.
(2 restaurants, bar)

Kowloon

Ambassador Nathan/Middle Rd. tel. 3-666321
At the head of Nathan Road, close to shops and nightclubs, a friendly hotel
with 320 rooms, $350-480 double.
(3 restaurants, bar, nightclub)

Astor 11 Carnarvon Rd. tel. 3-667261
In the heart of Tsim Sha Tsui's nightlife and shopping, a hotel which is
comfortable and reasonably priced with 148 rooms at $280 double.
(2 restaurants, bar)

Empress 17 Chatham Rd. tel. 3-660211
Convenient to downtown Kowloon and the airport with 189 rooms. Rates are
$380 double.
(2 restaurants)

Fortuna 355 Nathan Rd. tel. 3-851011
In busy Mongkok area, catering to Southeast Asian groups with 195 rooms,
good food and rates of $280-295 double.
(3 restaurants) (business centre) '

Grand 14 Carnarvon Rd. tel. 3-669331
In the centre of the entertainment area, a good reliable hotel with 194 rooms
at $200-420 double.
(2 restaurants, bar)

Holiday Inn Golden Mile 50 Nathan Rd. tel. 3-693111
On the shoppers' 'golden mile', a superbly run hotel with good bars and
restaurants and 650 rooms at $440-560 double.
(3 restaurants, bars, business centre, pool, sauna)

Holiday Inn Harbour View 70 Mody Road. tel. 3-7215161
New in East Kowloon, with good views of the harbour, the hotel has first class
food and 600 rooms at $550-690 double.
(3 restaurants, bar, pool, health club, business centre)

Hong Kong 3 Canton Rd. tel. 3-676011
A favourite with business visitors next to the Ocean Terminal and Star Ferry,
the hotel has superior food and 790 rooms at $410-660 double.
(3 restaurant, 4 bars, pool, health club)

Hyatt Regency 67 Nathan Rd. tel. 3-662321
Lively and efficient, a hotel close to the Kowloon action. Known for Hugo's restaurant, it has 776 rooms at $360-780 double.
(3 restaurants, 3 bars, nightclub, business centre)

International 33 Cameron Rd. tel. 3-663381
Convenient and comfortable, a hotel long known for moderate prices, it has 91 rooms at $280-360 double.
(restaurant, bar)

Marco Polo Tower III, Harbour City, Canton Rd.
A member of the Peninsula Group, with 440 rooms at $420 double.
(3 restaurants, bar, pool, health centre, sports centre)

Miramar 134 Nathan Rd. tel. 3-681111
A city within a city, a hotel with three wings and numerous facilities, the hotel has 1198 rooms at $440-700 double. (The old wing is to close 1983.)
(11 restaurants, 5 bars, theatre, supperclub, business centre, convention centre)

Nathan 378 Nathan Rd. tel. 3-885141
An unpretentious hotel at the top of the 'golden mile', the hotel is convenient and inexpensive with 122 rooms at $280 double.
(restaurant, bar)

New World New World Centre, 22 Salisbury Rd. tel. 3-6941111
On the edge of Kowloon bay next to a vast new shopping and entertainment complex, the hotel has 735 rooms at $310-480 double and good public facilities.
(3 restaurants, bar, pool)

Park 61 Chatham Rd. tel. 3-661371
An old favourite for its large rooms and comfortable bar-lounge, the hotel is well located. It has 450 rooms at $340-450 double.
(2 restaurants, bar)

Peninsula Salisbury Rd. tel. 3-666251
The grande dame of Hong Kong hotels with its famous lobby and fabled restaurants, the Pen has 340 rooms at $640-960 double.
(3 restaurants, bar, lobby lounge, business centre)

Regal Meridien East Tsim Sha Tsui
A member of the Air France-Meridien chain, this 601-room hotel has 450 rooms at $550-630 double.

Regal Meridien Kai Tak Airport
Hong Kong's first airport hotel has 403 rooms at $300-370 double.

Regent Salisbury Rd. tel. 3-7211211
A hotel with royal box views of the harbour, a breathtaking lobby lounge, superb restaurants and 605 rooms at $580-800 double.
(5 restaurants, bars, lobby lounge, pool, health club, business centre)

Royal Garden East Tsim Sha Tsui tel. 3-7215215
A member of the Mandarin International group, opening late 1981, it features a huge garden atrium lobby. With 436 rooms rates are $450-630 double.
(Rooms overlook indoor garden)

Shamrock 223 Nathan Rd. tel. 3-662271
For budget travellers, this hotel is comfortable and convenient, with 150 rooms at $210-320 double.
(2 restaurants, bar)

Shangri-La East Tsim Sha Tsui tel. 3-72121111
A deluxe hotel managed by Westin, it has fabulous decor, a fine French restaurant and 719 rooms at $575-850 double.
(4 restaurants, bar, lobby lounge, pool, sauna, business centre)

Sheraton 20 Nathan Rd. tel. 3-691111
Overlooking the harbour and at the head of the 'golden mile', the hotel is noted for its business facilities and international cabarets. It has 922 rooms at $630 double.
(5 restaurants, disco, nightclub, 8 bars, pool, business centre)

N.B. Prices are subject to change without notice.

Index

A

Aberdeen Boat Club 79
Aberdeen Marina 79
Aberdeen 73, 76, 77
airport buses 21
airport 21, 22, 44, 85
alleys 36
ancestor worship 17
animals 21
antiques 36
Ap Lei Chau 77
Arts Festival 52
Asian Antiques Fair 55
Asian Arts Festival 52

B

banks 23
bargaining 40
BBC 25
beach 47, 48, 92, 112
Bela Vista Hotel 100
bicycles 104
Blake Pier 88
bookstores 128
bridal gowns 114
Buddhism 17
bus tour 116
bus 25

C

Cable and Wireless 24
cameras 37
Camoes Museum 101
Cantonese 18
carry-on luggage 22
casino 100, 101
catty 65
Cheung Chau 62

Cheung Sha 112
children 45
China Products Stores 33
China 13, 16, 21, 103, 104, 109, 111
Chinese Arts and Crafts 33, 35
Chinese cooking 73
Chinese Street 117
Chiu Chow 68
chopsticks 65
Christianity 17
Chung Hom Kok 89
CITS 23
City Hall 88
climate 19, 20
clothing sizes 38
colonial cemetery 89
commune 109
communications 24, 42
computers 38
Confucianism 17
Connaught Centre 88
Consumer Council 33
craftsmen 76
credit cards 23
Cross-Harbour Tunnel 25, 42, 44, 87
cruise ships 21, 84
cultural performances 52
customs 21, 40

D

dancing 58
department stores 36
diamonds 33
dim sum 66
dinner theatre 53
disco 57, 58
dollar 23
Dragon Boat Festival 64
drugs 21, 45

E

Eastern Corridor 85
endangered species 21
English 18
exchange rates 23

F

factories 36
Fanling 49
ferries 21, 28, 88
festivals 60
fireworks factories 104
fishing 48
Flagstaff House 93
floor numbers 45
Food Street 114
food 64, 97
fortune-teller 76, 96, 121
Fung Ping Shan Museum 53
Furama Hotel 88

G

gambling 97, 100
geography 13
gods 121
gold 37
golf 47, 49
government 16
Grand Prix 100
Guia Lighthouse 104
Gurkhas 88
gwailo 17

H

Han Suyin 116
happy hour 56
Happy Valley Race Course 87
harbour 81
Hash House Harriers 125
health 22, 24, 98

herbal medicines 114
hiking 49, 92
HKTA 33, 41, 53
holidays 20
Hong Kong Cricket Club 89
Hong Kong Tennis Club 89
Hongkong Bank 113
Hopewell Centre 87
horse-racing 49, 87
hospitality 17
hostess clubs 58
hotels 22, 41
humidity 20
Hung Hom 85

I

ice skating 51
immigrants 16
Immigration Department 85
immigration 20

J

jade market 116
jade 38, 116, 117
jai alai 100
jazz 60
jetfoil 97
jewellery 37
Ji Fung 48
Jockey Club 49
jogging 49
Jumbo 77, 79, 80
junks 48

K

Kai Tak 21, 85

L

La Ronda 81, 93
Land Between, The 109

language 18
Lantau Peak 112
Lantau Tea Garden 111
Lantau 111
Lei Cheng Uk Branch Museum 53
Lei Cheng Uk 13
Lei Yue Mun 72
lion dance 62
Lo Wu 32
Lok Ma Chau 109
luggage 22
Luk Kwok Hotel 87
lunar New Year 20

M

Macau Ferry Pier 98
Macau 13, 20, 42, 88, 96, 111
mail 24
Man Mo Temple 120, 123, 124
Mandarin 18
market 77
Mass Transit Railway 29, 42
metro 29
money 23
movies 53
Murray Building 113
Murray House 93
Museum of Art 93
Museum of History 53
museums 53, 93, 96

N

Nathan Road 84
New Territories 109
New World Centre 84
New Year 20
newspapers 25
nightlife 44, 56
Noon Day Gun 87
North Point 85, 113

O

Ocean Park 73, 80
Ocean Terminal 84
open markets 36
opera 52, 55
opium 14
orchestra 52
Outward Bound 48

P

paintings 53
Peak Tower 76
Peak Tram 30
Peak 73
Peking 68
Peninsula Hotel 80, 84
personal cheques 23
Pien King 95
pirating 38
plants 21
Po Lin Monastery 111
Po Toi 72
police 18
Poor Man's Night Club 88
population 13, 14, 17
porcelain 38
Portuguese food 103
Pousada de Sao Tiago 100
pub 57, 58, 93
public light bus 28

Q

Queen Elizabeth Stadium 52

R

radio 25
railway 21, 32, 44, 109
rainfall 19
refugees 14, 16
Regent Hotel 80, 84

religion 17
Repulse Bay 89
restaurants 66
rickshaw 32
riots 14

S

sailing 47
sampan 77
schools 20
scuba diving 48
Sea Palace 79
seafood 65, 104
seasons 19
service charges 23
Shen Zhen 105
Shiqi 105, 108
shopping 32, 40, 44, 97
sightseeing 25, 41
Silvermine Bay 111, 112
Sok Kwu Wan 72
Space Museum 84
spectacles 37
St Paul's 101
Stanley Market 89
Stanley 89
Star Ferry 28, 42, 81, 84, 113
subway 29
Sung Dynasty Village 82, 95
swimming pools 44, 47
Szechuan 68

T

Tai Chi Chuan 51
Tai Pak 79
Taikoo Shing 85
tailors 37
Taipa 100
Tam Kung 17
Taoism 17
tap water 22
tax 17, 22

taxi 23, 25, 30
telephone 24
television 25, 53
Temple Street 120
temples 120
tennis 49
Ticketmate 97
Tiger Balm Gardens 116
Tin Hau Temple 92
Tin Hau 17
tipping 23
toilets 45
Tong Fuk Store 112
topless 60
train 32, 109
tram 29, 112
trotting 104
Tsim Sha Tsui East 85
tube 29
Tung Chung 112
typhoon 19

U

Up Club 125
Urban Council 16, 84

V

vegetarian lunch 111
vehicular ferry 84
Victoria Park 85, 114
visas 20

W

walking tour 116
walla-walla 28
Wan Fu 81
Wanchai 87, 113
Water 22
Wax Museum 96
winds 19
windsurfing 47, 48

Wong Tai Sin 120

Y
yachting 48
YMCA 44, 45
Yue Hwa 33
yum cha 66

Z
Zhuhai 105